Children Finding Faith

*Exploring
a child's response
to God*

Francis Bridger

Scripture Union

Scripture Union, 207–209 Queensway, Bletchley, MK2 2EB, England.

© Francis Bridger 2000

ISBN 1 85999 3230 (SU)
ISBN 1 902041 100 (CPAS)

British Library Cataloguing-in-Publication Data
A catalogue record for this book is available from the British Library.

Cover design by ie design
Internal design by Sue Jackson
Illustrations by Helen Gale

Printed and bound in Great Britain by Creative Print and Design (Wales) Ebbw Vale.

Contents

Dedication for Revised Edition

For Jayden and Hasina, whose journey of faith has only just begun.

Acknowledgements

I am grateful to many people who have made the revised edition of this book possible. Especially crucial have been: Sarah Mayers at Scripture Union Publishing whose editorial patience deserves a pay rise; Terry Larm of Fuller Theological Seminary, Pasadena who came to my rescue with a spare laptop at a critical moment when my own broke down; and my Australian brothers and sisters who have taught me a great deal about children and faith over the years. Without them all I'm not sure this project would have come to fruition.

Francis Bridger
February 2000

Preface to the
second edition

This revised edition of *Children Finding Faith*, twelve years after the publication of the original, is written with an even greater sense of urgency than the first. Numerous reports on children, young people and the church in this period tell the same story: the Millennium generation is even more alienated from organised religion than its predecessors. One statistic makes the point: in 1979, some 960,000 ten to nineteen year olds attended church regularly. By 1989 this same group had become 490,000 twenty to twenty-nine-year-olds – a 49% drop. In other words, the number of children and young people actively involved in Christian churches is diminishing at an alarming rate.[1] A report published in January 2000 even spoke of the church as 'one generation from extinction'.

The church needs children's evangelism, therefore, like never before. For if it fails to engage with the generation now being born, the future is bleak. And, as the figures show, there is no time to be lost. I hope that this book may play some small part in the urgent task that lies ahead.

In the first edition, I advanced ideas which were new to many in the field of childrens' work, especially those who – like me – identify with an Evangelical theological tradition. To my surprise, these ideas caused something of a stir. What in my innocence I had supposed to be no more than an exposition of thinking I had found exciting and relevant, to others proved revolutionary – even heretical.

Now, more than a decade on, I have rewritten some of the earlier material, kept other parts intact and added several new chapters. Comparison between the two editions will reveal that I have removed discussions on the role of theology, the family, the fatherhood of God and the incarnation. This is not because I have changed my mind or have come to regard these issues as irrelevant: far from it. In an ideal publishing world, I would retain these chapters. However, other – more pressing – questions have arisen and in the limited space available I have sought to address these rather than repeat earlier material. It remains my hope that the excised material may one day find its way (suitably revised) into a further book on ministry to children.

So what is new to this edition of *Children Finding Faith?* As before, the book divides into two parts. The first looks at how faith is born, develops and grows, using insights from faith development theorists such as John Westerhoff and James Fowler. But before this, I offer a substantial discussion of the kind of world in which children in the West are currently growing up. This is intended to make clear that youngsters, increasingly estranged from the Christian faith, do not come to the gospel as empty vessels or blank slates but as individuals who have already been exposed to a variety of influences and worldviews which have already predisposed them one way or another towards the Christian message. In other words, they are creatures shaped by the culture in which we live, and it is as such creatures that they hear and interpret the good news of Jesus Christ. To use a metaphor, it is crucial that we understand the nature of the baggage they bring with them before we seek to relieve them of it and present Christ as an alternative. This is the central message of chapter 1.

Chapters 2, 3 and 4 incorporate much of what was in the 1988 edition with some important additions. In the first edition I adopted (rather more uncritically than I should) views about children and the Bible that were close to those of the educationalist Ronald Goldman. In consequence, I was more cautious about the use of miracle stories and parables than I am now. Having read Roger and Gertrude Gobbel's book *The Bible: A Children's Playground*, I am persuaded that my caution was misplaced. The reader will therefore find several passages rewritten in these chapters which present a much modified view from that of 1988.

In part, this has arisen from an increasing awareness on my part, of the role played by imagination in the genesis and development of faith. Human beings – especially children – are incredibly imaginative and creative; and it is through the exercise of imagination that we find ourselves often led into new understandings and truths. Put another way, God has revealed himself in scripture in all kinds of ways that are enriched by a prayerful use of the imagination. He has not spoken simply in propositions but in metaphors, images, stories and visions. In short, he has spoken *imaginatively and creatively*. For those like me who were reared on the epistles of Paul and the belief that God has spoken through words rather than images, this is both liberating and revolutionary. It is not without risks – since giving the imagination free reign without theological and biblical boundaries can lead into all sorts of quicksands. But undoubtedly the risk is worth it, as I have sought to show. Chapters 2 – 4 therefore introduce new material on imagination, faith and play which I hope the reader will find useful even if he or she doesn't agree with it.

Part one is completed, as before, by a review of what it means to be a Millennium teenager. Had time and space allowed, I would have wished to allocate more time to the latest research into teenage attitudes to religion and values and although some of this is included, it is less than I would have wished. Again, a further book beckons…

Part two contains the most substantial changes. It presents a theological framework within which faith development insights should be set. Chapter 6 revisits the issues of sin and accountability and is substantially the same chapter as in the first edition.

Chapter 7 deals with the subject of conversion and faith development. Once more, evangelical readers may find this sits uncomfortably with the tradition of understanding conversion as an event rather than a process. I hope my exposition of Westerhoff and Fowler will reassure them that it is possible to see conversion as both. Moreover, by the addition of new material on James Loder's concept of 'the transforming moment', it is my intention that the role of imagination in bringing about change in a person's life may supply further insight into how God works to engender saving faith.

Chapter 8 is completely new and looks at the twin notions of believing and belonging – a distinction that has played a significant part in new thinking about evangelism in the 1990s. It argues that the traditional goals of evangelistic endeavour, bringing people to belief in Jesus, then enabling them to belong to a community of faith, should be considered in reverse: belong then believe.

Part two is then concluded with appendices which address two controversial issues: children and worship (especially Holy Communion) and children and spiritual gifts. The first of these chapters (Children, worship and Communion) is completely fresh and attempts to get behind the 'how to' questions, to theological principles. But because the problem of children in Communion has become increasingly pressing in recent years, I have focused much of the discussion in this chapter on that issue. The arguments may therefore seem to some readers provocative and uncomfortable. I hope this will not cause them to skip over it but instead will spur them on to engage with the point of view it puts forward. It is my hope that the unusual format of the chapter may encourage this.

Finally, Appendix 2 returns to the thorny issue of children and spiritual gifts. Having read what I wrote in the original edition of *Children Finding Faith*, one theological student commented in her degree dissertation that: 'I wonder whether this is part of the typically evangelical separation of components of faith into suitable/unsuitable for children?' I'm not sure she is right about the separation of components being typically evangelical but I certainly would want to argue that there are some things inappropriate to children and that in an age which is extremely sensitive to child abuse in all its forms, subtle and unsubtle, we must strive to avoid any hint of emotional or spiritual manipulation. The suitable/unsuitable dichotomy, in my view, is not only theologically grounded but pragmatically necessary.

Looking back, I recognise that the position I have taken on a number of topics may not be shared by all readers. For that reason, some may wish to consult books mentioned in the footnotes to discover alternative views. Indeed, in this revised version of *Children Finding Faith*, as with the original, I have found myself travelling something of a journey as I have researched and written it. Whether readers agree or disagree with what I have written, my hope is that it will enlarge our vision for relevance of the gospel to the millions of children who are already members of the Millennium generation. They need the love of Christ every bit as much as the rest of us and the evangelistic task is urgent.

And finally...

There remains one further issue which underlies all that is written in the chapters that follow. It is an issue which does not readily fit into either part one or part two and I have therefore (perhaps somewhat awkwardly) placed it here. But it is of such importance that we cannot ignore it, especially in an age that is highly sensitive to the vulnerability of children. The issue is that of child protection and the use of adult power. By considering it at this point, we shall be in a better position to inform our thinking as the book proceeds.

The nature of adult power

Power is not simply something that 'happens'. It has a structure and can be analysed. To do so enables us to understand and address the issue of adult power as it relates to children. The American pastoral theologian Ray S Anderson draws our attention to five types of power:[2]

- Exploitative power
- Manipulative power
- Competitive power
- Nutritive power
- Integrative power

Child abuse in any form takes place when the first three types are at work. The adult who seeks to exercise power over, or in competition with, children in his care is misusing the relationship he has with them. In an evangelistic context, the temptation to do so (whether conscious or unconscious) is enormous. For who does not want children to come to faith in Christ? The issue is: why do we want this and how?

This is where the fourth and fifth types of power are relevant. Nutritive power is concerned with building a person up: with nourishing them in their walk with Christ and their relationships with others. It is wholly positive. If our aim is to use our power towards children in this fashion, we are not seeking to abuse but to encourage. Similarly, the goal of integrative power is to make whole: to enable someone to bring together the disparate parts of their life. Like nutritive power, it is beneficent.

But how can we safeguard against allowing these positive types of power to degenerate into abusive ones? I would suggest the following guiding principles:[3]

1. *Respect*. This is absolutely fundamental. If we truly care for children we shall accord them respect. We shall see them not as fodder for our own wishes but as individuals in their own right. We shall not regard them as means to our ends but as ends in themselves. Children (or anybody else for that matter) do not exist to satisfy us: rather, we are called to serve *them*.

2. *Autonomy.* Just as much as adults, children are individuals made in the image of God, with the gift of freedom he has bestowed. To be sure, they are still maturing but this does not invalidate the theological as well as developmental truth that adults have a responsibility to encourage children in learning to exercise their God-given freedom. This means we shall hold back from pushing them in the spiritual direction we want them to take simply because we believe we know best. We are back to the issue of respect.

3. *Self-critical discernment.* It takes wisdom to know the way in which God may be leading a child. In addition to being prayerful, the children's worker will want to seek God for the ability to discern what is appropriate at any given moment. Essential to this is the quality of openness. On one hand, we shall need to be open to God in such a way that we genuinely are ready to do whatever he wants (which may conflict with our own inclinations) and on the other to be open to hearing what the child in front of us is saying. Both kinds of openness will in turn require us to know ourselves well and to be willing to recognise when we are thinking and acting out of our own desires, whims or prejudices. In short, we have to be prepared to ask ourselves whether we have a hidden agenda we are seeking to smuggle in, and even more to admit we can be wrong.

4. *Beneficence* implies a very practical judgement: what will achieve the greatest good? How can I act to promote this child's best interests? These are the key questions. Moreover, in its negative form, it asks the question: 'how can I avoid doing harm?'. And, when faced with a situation involving children, this question is always necessary. But stated positively, the principle of beneficence points us towards acting for positive good.

Here Anderson's analysis of power becomes useful once more. For the goal of positive good will require us to ask whether any proposed action will be more likely to fall into the category of exploitative, manipulative or competitive power on one hand, or the category of nutritive or integrative power on the other. There should be no doubt that for those who work with children (as indeed with young people or adults) that nutritive and integrative power remain the only kinds that should be contemplated.

Coming to terms with the realities of power relationships is crucial, then, if we are to grasp what it means to work with children. For children regard adults as all-powerful – a fact that gives adults enormous power over them. It is essential therefore, that as we consider how faith develops and the issues surrounding evangelism among children, we ask ourselves the hard questions about our use of power. Not to do so would be to fail those whom we seek to serve.

Notes to Preface:

1 Phil Moon, 'Church Demographics' in Leslie J Francis, William K Kay, Alan Kerby and Olaf Fogwill (eds), *Fast-moving Currents in Youth Culture*, Oxford, Lynx, 1995.

2 Ray S Anderson, *The Soul of Ministry*, Louisville, Kentucky, John Knox Press, 1997, pp151–2.

3 These principles are based on standard codes of practice for pastoral counselling, designed to protect those seeking professional help at a time of emotional disturbance. They are also applicable to those who work with children in any kind of ministry. See Association of Christian Counsellors, *Code of Ethics*. Also, Tim Bond, *Standards and Ethics for Counselling in Action*, London, Sage Publications 1995.

Part One

CHILDREN, DEVELOPMENT AND FAITH

Modern views of the way faith
develops throughout a child's life.

1 What kind of world?

The cultural context of faith development

Welcome to Clumber Street! Set in the imaginary suburb of Anytown, 'The Street', as it is known to its inhabitants, is a cul-de-sac containing a typical cross-section of ordinary people. It's a microcosm of any town or suburb in the Western world today. Indeed, it could be *your* street or mine.

But suppose we were to look at the residents of Clumber Street a little more closely. What would we find? That's exactly what we're going to do. Because as we discover more about them, we'll begin to put together a picture of the kind of world in which the Millennium generation is growing up and of the worldviews with which they are surrounded.

Let's start at number 1. The first thing we notice is that it's empty. The residents – Mike and Jo – moved out last week. They were a nice, friendly, young couple married two years ago. Clumber Street was their first married home, although they had lived together at number 1 for a year with their baby son Tyler before the wedding. Now they've moved to a larger house a few miles away.

Interestingly, number 1 is typical of Anytown in that it symbolises the fact that Anytown is a place of constant change: people moving in and out; businesses closing down and starting up; new shops and leisure pursuits – life never stays still. Some of the older residents hark back to the 'good old days' when nothing ever changed (or at least that's the way it now seems). But for the Millennium generation, change is a way of life.

Lined up to come into number 1 are the Watts family: Lenny, Dawn and their two children Delia and Sam. They are a bit nervous about moving into a white, middle-class area since they are black and have suffered prejudice – both intentional and unintentional – in their respective jobs. But Clumber Street is handy for Lenny's and Dawn's work and they have heard good reports about the schools. So they're determined to make a go of it and are looking forward to moving in next week.

Next door at number 3 live the Porters. Bel (Belinda) and Andy (Andrew) are in their early thirties with twin children – Craig and Lisa, aged nine. It's a very busy household since Bel and Andy are both teachers: Bel is Head of Music at Anytown High School; while Andy is Deputy Principal at a college half an hour away.

Not only are Bel and Andy busy, so are Craig and Lisa. Craig takes after his mother and is keen on music (he plays four instruments). He's involved in all sorts of out-of-school activities ranging from weekly guitar lessons to playing in a band. Lisa, meanwhile, has a lively interest in astronomy and has joined the Anytown Skywatchers (Junior Division).

Number 3, then, is a home that is constantly on the go. Someone is always busy with something. Life is like a constantly spinning tumble-dryer.

The residents of number 5 couldn't be more different. George and Mildred Owen are in their late seventies, taking life easy. George retired from factory work fifteen years ago and hasn't regretted it a bit. Mildred has hardly worked in paid employment at all, since she spent most of her adult life as a housewife looking after George and their three children who have now moved away. Indeed, they're scattered throughout the country. The nearest, David, lives just over 100 miles distant.

To all intents and purposes, then, Clumber Street is George and Mildred's family. They are the street's oldest inhabitants, having moved in forty years ago when it was first built. They have seen generations come and go. For them, Clumber Street is a living community and they are its elders. They find their identity there.

At number 7 lives Rachel Symons, a lone parent bringing up her son James (12). Rachel was divorced from her former husband, Alan, six years ago. The divorce was very messy and left a great deal of bad feeling. Alan has since remarried but sees James once a week.

Rachel is lonely and wishes she had another adult in her life. But since Alan there has been nobody else. The pain of her divorce left Rachel unconfident and distrustful of relationships with men. She lavishes all her energy and affection on James.

James, however, *does* have a love of his life – sport. He's fanatical about all team games but especially football and basketball. At five feet eleven inches, he's obviously going to be tall, which suits his ambitions perfectly: he wants to play international basketball for England. And although he doesn't know it yet, talent scouts have already had their eyes on him as he has represented his school in national championships. James is 150 per cent committed to sport.

Next to Rachel and James live the McDonalds. Or to be accurate, Barry McDonald and Sarah Wilson. Although not married, everyone thinks of them as if they are and calls them by Barry's surname. Barry and Sarah don't mind this. They regard themselves as good as married since they're committed to each other and to their three children: Hayley (10), William (9) and Kerry (7).

Barry is a biochemist who works as a researcher for an international pharmaceutical conglomerate. Sarah is a local doctor. All their children have been brought up to be interested in science and to see it as *the* instrument of human progress. Hayley wants to follow her mother into medicine; William is determined to become an astronaut; and Kerry just likes playing with test tubes. They are all avid fans of *Star Trek* and computer games.

A bit further along the street live Brian, Zoe and Natalie. They're aged between nineteen and twenty-one and are students at Anytown University. They share the house and the rent. But although similar in age, that's where the likeness stops: they're completely different personalities.

Brian is quiet, studious and hard-working. He is studying economics and wants to work for an international oil company when he graduates. He has a small circle of friends who are equally committed to getting good jobs. Zoe thinks he's a bit of a nerd (but then she thinks anyone who works is a nerd).

Zoe is the opposite to Brian. She's loud, extrovert and totally focused on having a good time. She's the complete pleasure seeker, enjoying wild parties, alcohol, recreational drugs and, of course, sex. Zoe doesn't think about the future – there's too much fun to be had in the present. She's simply a hedonist.

Natalie, on the other hand, is ambitious like Brian and enjoys a good time but is nowhere near as wild as Zoe. She has chosen her course – media studies – with great care for she believes the media hold the key to the future. She doesn't want *any* job in the media – she wants a *top* job.

More permanent at number 13 are the Watkinson family. They are an interesting mix. Phil is 49 and married to Ruth who is a few years younger. He is a self-employed financial adviser. Ruth is a dentist. Both have been married before: Phil to Jackie who died in a road accident seven years ago; and Ruth to Dennis who left her for another woman six years back.

When Phil and Ruth got married last year, they brought with them their respective children. At 14, Alice is Phil's youngest daughter (his other daughter has left home and lives in America). She is fiery and committed to good causes. Her current passion is environmentalism. Her friends joke with her about being a 'tree hugger'.

Ben is Ruth's son. He is 17, thoughtful and romantic at heart (although he's still shy with girls) and sincerely committed to a number of New Age beliefs. Ben's sister Amy (16), however, disagrees with him. She is a committed Christian who worships at a lively church nearby. It has lots of young people and she feels at home there. Recently, she has been trying to get Ben to see the error of his ways but with little success. She's not sure what to do next but plans to talk to her pastor about how to witness more effectively at home.

One door along, number 15, is where Ron and Jill Callaghan live. They run a small business which occupies much of their time. They have no children (no one is quite sure why, though there have been rumours). Now in their late fifties, Ron and Jill keep themselves to themselves, and although they have lived in Clumber Street for eight years, hardly anyone knows them beyond being able to pass the time of day. None of the neighbours has ever been in their house for any reason whatsoever.

Ron and Jill like it that way. They don't see why others should have access to their private world. But even the least observant outsider could get some idea of their lifestyle by observing number 15 from across the street.

Such a person would quickly spot that Ron and Jill's house is very expensive indeed. Everything about it cries 'consumption' – from the well-appointed exterior to the luxury cars in the driveway. What's more, if they could see further, they would notice all the signs of affluence: gold taps in the bathroom, a jacuzzi, a sauna in the back garden, top-of-the range kitchen fittings and appliances, en-suite bedrooms, a home cinema system – the lot! No expense has been spared to give Ron and Jill what they call 'the good life'.

And so we come to the last two houses in the street, numbers 17 and

19. At 17 you'll find Derek Turnbull. He's a single man in his twenties who works as a computer programmer. In fact, computers are his whole life. He lives, breathes and eats computers. Derek's an IT fanatic. He has three PCs of his own, including the latest laptop with every conceivable gizmo. He also has a palmtop that doesn't only tell the time of day in 14 countries simultaneously but can also double as a mobile phone, fax and e-mail link.

Needless to say, Derek's on the Internet (he even has his own website). He has friends all over the world whom he's never met but has chatted to hundreds of times via e-mail. His phone bill would be phenomenal if he didn't work for a communications company who provide him with unlimited call time. For Derek, computers *are* his world.

Oddly enough, Derek isn't a complete loner. He has made efforts to build friendships in Clumber Street. The trouble is he only has one topic of conversation – computers. This is fine for five or even ten minutes but not for hours on end. Consequently, although Derek wants to make friends, he finds it hard.

Finally there's number 19. Here live Linda Jackson and Ellen DeVere. Both are in their early forties and have a lesbian relationship. Ellen (who has only recently admitted to herself that she's gay) has two children living with her by her earlier marriage: Clark (14) and Lois (12). Ellen is a P.A. to a wealthy businessman; Linda is a successful lawyer. They are currently considering fostering or adopting a hard-to-place child and have been encouraged in this by their discussions with social workers from the local authority social services department.

At first, Linda and Ellen were nervous about 'coming out' to their friends and neighbours. But the residents of Clumber Street are a pretty tolerant lot. Apart from George and Mildred who find it hard to understand or condone Linda and Ellen's relationship, the general attitude is one of 'live-and-let-live'. Provided Linda and Ellen's relationship doesn't impinge on anyone else's life, people are happy to regard their sexuality as a purely private matter.

So much for fictional Anytown. If you watch soap operas, you'll quickly recognise in this sketch of Clumber Street a typical soap technique: the representation of society as a whole by a small group of characters located in a single, small community. As with all good soaps, the characters and their situations serve to typify the extremes of what we would find on a much broader canvas. In that sense, Clumber Street is very untypical. It's unlikely that we would find such a combination in many cul-de-sacs in middle suburbia. But this is done for a purpose: the pen pictures of the residents supply vital clues as to the main features of modern life. Taken together, they act as a microcosm of contemporary society. And in doing so, they make it comprehensible.

In Clumber Street, for example, we observe (not in order of importance):

- the centrality of change in modern life;
- the busy-ness of life;
- the nuclear family no longer the only type of family;
- a range of types of family life;
- marriage as a lifestyle option;
- cohabitation as an accepted alternative;
- divorce and remarriage as a common experience;
- the dominance of computers and information technology;
- confident assumptions about science and progress;
- 'pick 'n' mix' moral and religious beliefs where all views and practices are regarded as equally valid provided they don't interfere with the choices of others;
- sexuality regarded as a purely private matter;
- the idolisation of individual choice;
- the pursuit of pleasure as a legitimate goal in itself;
- belief in material acquisition as a way of life.

The proclamation of faith in Christ doesn't take place in a vacuum but rather has to contend with a cultural worldview already delivered and which has already taken root.

This not-quite-random collection serves to illustrate the complex world into which the Millennium generation is being born. But it does more than that. It enables us to glimpse something of the worldview (or views) that surround them from birth. In fact, without realising it, the Clumber Street folk in their own ways all place their faith in something, whether family, science, wealth, computers or whatever. They each hold beliefs and practices that give meaning, purpose and a sense of ultimacy to their lives: in short, the sort of faith held when the traditional Christian view of God is pretty well left out of the picture. And it's this secular version of faith that the majority of our children absorb from the moment they enter the world. Once we understand this, we begin to see that the proclamation of faith in Christ doesn't take place in a vacuum but rather has to contend with a cultural worldview already delivered and which has already taken root.

The task of the evangelist must therefore be to *understand* something of this worldview before she points to the reality and truth of the gospel. Before we can convert the world we must first comprehend it.

Contemporary culture

So far we have used the example of Clumber Street to highlight a number of features of everyday life. But there exists a wider picture we need to grasp if we are to build the foundations for effective evangelism. This picture affects children and adults alike but is especially important in understanding the formation of children. It is a sketch of contemporary *culture*.

In what follows I am going to speak primarily of *Western* culture. This is not because it should be regarded as somehow superior to others or more blessed by God. (Indeed, it would be possible to argue convincingly that the West has drifted far from God and is dangerously liable to judgment. But that's a different topic...) Rather, what follows will concentrate on Western culture because (a) I would feel it presumptuous to speak about non-Western cultures since I have little experience of them; and (b) this book is addressed in the first instance to those who either live within Western culture or a society influenced by the West.

There is one more thing to be said before launching into a survey of those larger forces that are shaping – and will continue to shape – the outlook of the Millennium generation. Contemporary culture has been described as postmodern. While I accept the term as a useful label to characterise certain features of Western culture, I have avoided using it as much as possible. This is partly because the notion of postmodernity is highly contested but also because this particular piece of jargon is not always helpful. So in general, for 'postmodern' read 'contemporary'. We shouldn't get hung up on the term – it's the features that we need to recognise.

A contented culture

The culture represented by Clumber Street is the richest and most powerful in history. Science, technology and modern economics have produced an unprecedented period of economic growth and well-being. From the standpoint of material prosperity, we enjoy a standard of living our forbears would never have dreamt of.

One consequence of this has been the rise of what the American economist J K Galbraith has called 'the culture of contentment.' By this he means that Western culture has now become so prosperous and comfortable that it basks in the belief that it has achieved the good life without end. Of course, there are pockets of poverty, even in rich societies, but progress will ensure that they are temporary and limited. Surrounded by technological advance, political stability, economic growth, universal education and health care, those who live in the West, or who have successfully imitated its development, can rest safe in their contentment. Compared to past generations, we have never had it so good.

But, according to Galbraith, there is a further, disturbing, aspect. In such a culture there is little need for commitment to great moral causes or indeed to anything other than the good life. Economic and political liberty have been achieved. The reasons for the great revolutions of the past – poverty and oppression – have been conquered. For the majority of the population, there is nothing left to fight for except to hold onto contentment. Moral indignation is left to the eco-warriors and animal liberationists on the fringes of society. Most people have neither time nor inclination to get involved with moral campaigns.

The culture of contentment is also ambivalent about God. Its achievements have been won without him. When asked their views by opinion pollsters, the majority will say they believe in God, but when pressed have little idea of what they mean. Certainly they hold no truck with organised religion; nor are they willing to commit themselves to anything more than a threadbare acknowledgment that some kind of supreme Being probably exists. Commitment and Christian discipleship are pooh-poohed as irrelevant. The reality of life consists in acquiring and consuming material things, looking after one's own, and generally enjoying the short span we have on this planet. God is at the margins or nowhere to be seen, except perhaps in life crises such as birth, marriage and death. Then he may get a look in. Most of the time he is treated as absent.

> *The society which has piled up material well-being beyond the dreams of any previous civilisation, finds itself with a spiritual hole in its heart.*

This, at least, is one side of the story. But, as we shall see, there is another, and it is this other side that makes the attitude of contemporary culture ambivalent. For the society which has piled up material well-being beyond the dreams of any previous civilisation, finds itself with a spiritual hole in its heart and has begun once more to ask questions about meaning and purpose – questions which are essentially religious.

This same society, however, will have little to do with the institutional church. It is willing to talk in terms of 'the spiritual' but not in terms of religion. Hence it remains ambivalent about God. It senses there is something missing that ever-increasing wealth cannot supply; but it is unwilling to return to the God of previous generations. Instead, it indulges in pick 'n' mix beliefs where individuals simply pick what they want from a variety of sources – even a variety of religions – and mix them all together until they arrive at the dish they desire.

Sarah Ferguson, the Duchess of York, illustrates this perfectly. In October 1998 she began hosting a series of daytime TV chat show programmes in the U.K. Here is how a commentator in the London *Times* described it: 'the Duchess of York confided to us, in her introduction, that her personal recipe for spirituality consisted of taking bits from various religions and mixing them together – a process she compared to that of mixing ingredients to make a cake...'. Noting that not all ingredients would necessarily mix well, the writer couldn't resist pursuing the analogy: 'viewers with long and excitable memories probably couldn't help but wonder if Sarah Ferguson's cake was maybe half baked.'

Behind the joke is a serious point: pick 'n' mix spirituality might not be very coherent. But as long as it works, so what? In contemporary culture, the test of faith is not whether it is true but whether it brings personal satisfaction – that is, whether it brings about contentment. This presents a unique challenge to traditional Christianity.

The evangelistic challenge is enormous – but so is the opportunity.

It's in such a society that the Millennium generation finds itself growing up. Children of this generation are being offered a more confused cultural worldview than was the case with their parents and grandparents, many of whom simply assumed that God was dead and that contentment was the be-all and end-all of human existence. But despite this confusion, the assumptions of the contentment culture pervade every aspect of our children's lives. There is no institution (except perhaps the church at its best) that is not riven with the philosophy of contentment. The worldview of the Millennium generation is being formed by its parents' belief that contentment is the ultimate life goal, with 'spirituality' as merely an aspect of contentment. The evangelistic challenge is enormous - but so is the opportunity.

A consumer culture

When we ask what makes the contentment culture content, the answer is simple: continuous consumption. Without it, Western societies would have no reason to exist. They would simply collapse. And with them would go the economies of the rest of the world. For the world economy is based upon the assumption of ever-rising living standards fuelled by the desire to consume. What's more, it is highly interdependent. It only needs consumption to falter in Europe, America or Asia and recession threatens governments around the globe.

But how is this relevant to a discussion of children finding faith? Remember we are trying to get a bird's-eye picture of the worldview which is drip-fed to our children from the earliest years of their lives: a set of beliefs and assumptions that shapes their understanding of reality from day one. It is nothing less than a version of faith – albeit a godless one. It is a worldview the gospel must subvert if there is to be room for Christ.

What attitudes within consumer culture does the gospel challenge? Firstly, the presumption that creation is given for human beings to manipulate and consume as they wish. This lies at the heart of consumerism. But it also flies in the face of a Christian understanding of the earth as created by God for his glory and only secondarily for human needs, let alone human wants. From the industrial revolution onwards, Western societies have acted as if they possessed an absolute right to exploit the world's resources (including its peoples) for their own satisfaction. Yet the biblical view is exactly the opposite: we are to live as stewards or custodians of God's creation. We are responsible to him for its care and upkeep. And we will be answerable to him for its destruction.

When we begin to think in these terms we see immediately that the cultural assumption of a right to consume lies in stark opposition to the way of Jesus, although in a consumerist society, this assumption is taken for granted and finds its way into our children's worldviews without question. One of the tasks of ministry among children, therefore, is to challenge this view at its roots and to enable young people to become critical of it. This will not be an easy task for them or for those who work among them. But, if we are to honour the truth of scripture and Christian faith, we must present youngsters with an alternative to the consumerist mentality that surrounds them.

Secondly, the gospel undermines the presumption that human beings lie at the centre of the universe. This article of faith (for that is what it is) is built into consumerism. What other justification can there be for the destruction of the environment that has taken place in the name of the right to consume? True, we are now beginning to see the rise of a world-wide reaction against human-centredness in the shape of the environmental movement. But even here there is ambiguity: to most people, environmentalism has taken centre stage not because it seeks to preserve the environment for its own sake but because our survival depends upon it. In other words, humanity remains all-important.

Once more, Christian teaching has something critical to say. Human beings are not at the centre of the universe. God is. Our concern for creation should arise out of our desire to care for the world he has given us, not because we fear for the future of our right to consume. Consumerism is wrong because it denies this fundamental truth.

Thirdly, Christian truth challenges the idolisation of choice. In contemporary culture, economic freedom is seen as a basic human right. The right to choose is the paramount value. The customer reigns supreme. The outcome is that in every walk of life (including church life) the right to choose is inbuilt. Individuals are seen first and foremost as if they are consumers possessing a natural right to have what they want. They are takers rather than givers.

Such an attitude is not consciously thought-out. It is the product of centuries of emphasis on the importance of the individual. Western culture is devoted to the belief that the individual is paramount. As one writer has put it: 'The final values of life begin and end with individuals and with the states or act of individuals.'[1]

The problem with this view is that by promoting the individual to an almost god-like status, culture has progressively chipped away at the equally profound truth that individuals cannot flourish without community. In John Macmurray's words, 'I need You in order to be myself'.[2] Or, to quote Kallistos Ware, 'My human being is a relational being. My personal unity is fulfiled in community.'[3]

Yet the philosophy of consumerism, with its absolute belief in choice, militates against community. It advocates the rights of individuals to choose (and spend) according to their individual desires, irrespective of the needs and considerations of others. The revival of faith in 'The Market' as a solution to economic problems at the end of the twentieth century has merely reinforced such individualism. The Millennium generation, by and large, assumes this to be a fact of life, a self-evidently 'good thing'.

The Australian social commentator Hugh Mackay notes that the emphasis on freedom of choice has its roots in, and is particularly strong among, those who were born in the 1970s and '80s. He calls this the 'Options generation'.[4] This group is particularly significant for our discussion because they are the parents of the Millennium generation. And like all parents, they will pass on their set of values to their children.

But Mackay points out a further crucial consequence: the central value held by the Options generation is that of being free to choose and, more importantly, being free to keep one's options open: to be able to opt in and out of activities or relationships as one wants without permanent or even long term commitment:

> 'Whether they are thinking about a course of study, a job, a sexual partner, a political party, a set of religious beliefs, or even whether they'll be home for dinner tonight, they have decided to remain as non-committal as possible for as long as possible.'[5]

The core value of adolescence, then, is freedom to choose (or freedom to hang loose) combined with absolute belief in the individual. It is one which the parents of the Millennium generation took for granted in their youth and which, consciously or unconsciously, they will pass onto their own children.

This poses a considerable challenge for evangelism for all kinds of reasons. The first is that the self-centred mindset of the Options mentality must be seen as truly anti-Christian. The gospel is concerned with self-*giving* (on the model of Jesus), not self-*getting*. We are to love our neighbours as well as ourselves. God has made us to be people-in-relationship rather than individuals out for themselves. Human beings have been created as individuals-in-community, designed to flourish as social beings in the image of God. It is not God's purpose that they should grow up as isolated individuals, each living in their own little world like modern Robinson Crusoes.

By contrast with contemporary cultural views, faith in Christ leads to the classic Christian virtues of self-renunciation, compassion and generosity to be found and practised in the context of community. Christian faith is a corporate faith not a purely individualistic one. But in the wake of the consumer revolution of the 1980s and 1990s, young people grow up surrounded by exactly the opposite philosophy: acquire, consume and look after number one. Evangelism which is genuinely biblical, therefore, will offer a radical alternative not as an optional add-on to personal salvation but as an integral part of Christian discipleship. The gospel is radical at this point or it is nothing.

A Sci-tech culture

Science and technology have made Western culture what it is. Without them, it would still be stuck in the Middle Ages. There would be no electricity, no gadgets, no mechanised transport, no modern medicine, no life-saving medical machinery. People would live shorter lives, afflicted by plagues and surrounded by suffering. The list is endless.

Few would argue with the view that science and technology have brought enormous progress. Indeed, the McDonald/Wilson household in Clumber Street revolves around an absolute belief in science. But this has been bought at a price. In the wake of scientific discovery and technological development have come previously unimaginable horrors. The self-same scientific and technological mindset that gave us economic, social and medical progress has also given us nuclear weapons, environmental disasters, the gulags and the holocaust. Even now, further technological nightmares lie just around the corner: genetic engineering of humans, cloning to order, 'superbugs' resistant to antibiotics – to mention but a few.

The Millennium generation therefore stands at a critical juncture in the development of scientific and technological culture. The future both beckons and repels. At one and the same time, technology offers itself as saviour and destroyer.

Science can address the how questions but it cannot deal with the why ones.

The young people of Clumber Street consequently represent a generation that relies on science but at the same time is ambivalent towards it. To be sure, they see no other way forward in terms of material progress and the conquest of disease, famine and premature death. But despite this, they are wary. Unlike their grandparents born half a century before, they don't have unlimited faith in science as the guarantor of the unending good life. Neither do they put their trust in technology's ability to solve all the world's problems. And unlike their parents born in the

1970s and '80s they are doubtful about the unquestioned assumption that technology is inherently good because it alone can deliver consumption and contentment.

At present, Hayley, William and Kerry McDonald have simply accepted their parents' uncritical worldview. But it would be interesting to know in 10 years time whether all three held the same beliefs, or whether, as they came to share some of the scepticism of their peers, they stopped believing. Like the rest of the Millennium generation, the McDonald children are at a crossroads.

In addition, the more thoughtful of the Millennium generation realise that while science can answer many questions, it cannot answer the deepest questions of all: Why are we here? What meaning can we give to human existence? What purpose does the universe hold? Science can address the *how* questions but it cannot deal with the *why* ones.

Of course, these issues are not very real during childhood years. But from about twelve years onwards, they will begin to surface. As children move through their teenage years to become young adults, they inevitably find questions of meaning and purpose more and more pressing. Alice, Ben and Amy Watkinson are instances of this.

But how will they answer such questions? A 1994 survey of 13,000 UK young people aged 13–15 revealed some interesting findings: 37% believed in ghosts, 35% in horoscopes, 31% in contacting spirits of the dead, 19% in the devil, 19% in fortune tellers and 18% in black magic.[6] This suggests a real confusion about spiritual issues. Science is not rejected absolutely but is set alongside belief in supernaturalism. As the authors of the report note (p162): 'Despite the scientific and technological basis of culture, there is evidence of beliefs in practices with a supernatural connection ... in other words, this is a scientific age with New Age overtones.' If this represents the cultural assumptions of the Millennium generation, the task of evangelism must be to understand and address them.

An IT culture

Of all the scientific/technological developments at the end of the twentieth century, the rapid expansion of information technology is probably the most mind-blowing and the one that contains the greatest potential for both good and evil. It is also the development with which the Millennium generation is most familiar. Whether we like it or not, IT (and the computers that have given rise to the phenomenon) governs our lives and will continue to do so.

We can see how true this is by imagining for a moment what might be a typical day in the lives of, say, the Porter or McDonald children, or perhaps the Watkinsons. They wake up at 7.00 am. How might they be woken? Craig Porter has a digital alarm clock/radio that switches on automatically and tunes into his favourite pre-programmed radio station. Hayley McDonald is woken by an alarm call from (guess what?) her personal palmtop computer. It, too, is programmed to send out an audio signal and also doubles as a notebook, diary and electronic organiser. It fits into her pocket and goes everywhere with her. Further along Clumber Street, James Symons logs onto the Internet to surf the sports websites.

Meanwhile back at the Porters, Craig's mum, Belinda, switches on the automatic washing machine and sets the timer on the electric oven to come on at 5.00 pm so that she doesn't forget (she has a busy day coming up). Both these appliances are controlled by microchips. As this is going on, Craig's dad, Andy, is rushing out of the door to get to work. He's running late so he grabs his mobile phone to make some calls while travelling to college.

At the McDonalds' house, Kerry is watching breakfast TV on one channel while video recording cartoons on another to watch later. Since they have a digital satellite dish which can get 100 channels, there's never any shortage of stuff to watch and record.

And so the day goes on. At school, Belinda Porter works on a report for the school governors, using one of the school's computers donated by a supermarket chain. Andy, meanwhile, is even later getting to work than he had expected since the signalling system further along the railway line has failed. It is controlled by computer.

In one of the classes at Anytown High, Belinda's son, Craig, is in a music lesson. He enjoys making music on an electronic keyboard just as much as he likes listening to CDs. His teacher always says she can't get over how much better these sound than the old 33 rpm records she used to buy when she was a child. Craig politely nods but doesn't have the faintest idea what she is talking about – 33s were p.c. (pre-computer).

And if all this were not enough evidence of a computer-driven life, we have only to think about what will happen after school and work to appreciate that our entire lives are organised around – and organised by

– activities that depend on computers: watching TV, playing Nintendo games, surfing the Net, going to the cinema, swimming pool or ice rink, eating at McDonalds – you name it, and it probably wouldn't be able to happen without a computer somewhere behind the scenes.

Even this cursory glance at a fictional day makes us realise how computer-centred we are. When we think also of how hospitals, transport, power stations – in fact every aspect of daily life – are dominated by computer technology, it becomes obvious that the Millennium generation is growing up in a world undreamt of when their parents were children.

> **Images bombard children from all directions so that their perceptions of reality are conditioned by the power of Image.**

An image culture

We live in a world dominated by images. Television, films, computers, virtual reality, theme parks – all are common features of the contemporary child's world. Images bombard children from all directions so that their perceptions of reality are conditioned by the power of image.

Imagine this, for example. You are watching TV with your 8-year-old son and 6-year-old daughter. Halfway through the programme the advertisements appear. As it's children's TV, all the commercials are child-centred. You groan because you know that you'll be lucky if your purse or wallet escapes the next three minutes unscathed. There will be a succession of images attempting to persuade you and your kids that you cannot afford to be without the advertised products, whether chocolate-covered cornflakes, Barbie and Ken or the latest Playstation game. The pressure to buy will be enormous. (So great is the power of the TV image that entire cable channels are devoted solely to 24 hour shopping. All the viewer has to do is to phone in the name and code number of the advertised item along with a credit card number and the product will be dispatched within hours.)

The power of images, though, is not confined to advertising. At every twist and turn we encounter the dominance of image. Take, for example, the use of the word 'icon' to denote someone who is held up as representative of a fashion, sport or trend. It is significant that the term is used at all, for icon derives from a Greek word literally meaning image. To say that somebody is an icon, therefore, reinforces the idea that all important aspects of our lives are best understood through image.

In a child's world this is terribly important. Individuals are held up as icons or role models for them to follow, whether it's a pop musician advocating support for good causes (think of Bob Geldof and Live Aid) or an ex-footballer advertising crisps. The point is still the same: icon=image=power.

This equation is highly seductive. In the first place, although advertising is the most blatant example, the substitution of image for argument is even more insidious. In a highly visual culture bombarded by the electronic media, children register the message conveyed by an image much more than one conveyed by rational explanation. Words become secondary; images primary. The power-holders in today's world are those who are able to wield the most effective images.

Secondly, as a number of writers have pointed out, images do not merely *describe* reality, they *interpret* it as well. And whoever acts as interpreter holds great power. This means that the media, who after all are the most important source of information in the contemporary world, possess enormous power over people's lives without most of us realising it.

The most worrying conclusion of this line of thought is that images are capable of being used not to inform and educate but to manipulate. Sometimes this is done intentionally. But, as often as not, manipulation happens unconsciously and without malice aforethought.

Take, for example, the effect of soap operas. They are central to the daily life of millions of children. They form the staple diet of peak time viewing. Indeed, *Neighbours* achieved its dominance precisely because the programme schedulers took the decision to screen it as the final segment of children's television at 5.35 pm after children had arrived home from school. As a result, at the time of writing, *Neighbours* is watched by something like 10 million each day – the equivalent of nearly two-thirds of the entire population of Australia, the country that produces it!

More important than mere numbers, however, is the effect of soaps on child viewers. They are uniquely powerful because they use story – the most potent of teaching methods – to: (a) send out messages about what is right and wrong; (b) provide examples through characters and situations; (c) define good and bad behaviour through the interaction of storylines and supposedly ordinary people; (d) present the hidden agendas of the writers.

This last point is particularly significant. It means that the beliefs and prejudices of the writers can be smuggled in without viewers realising what's going on. Behaviour or attitudes that would be regarded as doubtful or unacceptable if we encountered them in real life are made more plausible when presented in the setting of a soap opera.

> **In a highly visual culture bombarded by the electronic media, children register the message conveyed by an image much more than one conveyed by rational explanation.**

More often than not (since this is the essence of soaps) this process occurs in the context of sexual morality. Sex for pleasure rather than as a sign of lifelong commitment is portrayed as normal. Indeed, to think of a Christian view of sex as properly confined to marriage is seen at best as merely a lifestyle option and at worst as laughably out-of-date. Homosexual relationships are assumed to be equivalent to heterosexual ones. Cohabitation rather than marriage is the norm. And so on. Clumber Street is typical soapland. What's more, disagreement with such views is quickly dealt with by the simple device of avoiding rational discussion and putting contrary views in the mouths of characters who are no more than a joke. The message this sends to children is, from a Christian point of view, disastrous.

But it's in the area of religion that soaps send out the most subversive messages. Invariably, religious beliefs are portrayed as marginal, neurotic or hypocritical. The upshot is to create and sustain an impression that religious faith doesn't matter, is irrelevant to normal life and is the preserve of those who are either two-faced or unable to cope with reality. There are rare exceptions but this portrayal is the norm.

Once more we are faced with the massive power of image in a culture saturated with images. Children, exposed to images day after day, find themselves bombarded with messages most of which carry an anti- or sub-Christian worldview. This is the reality of the world in which the Millennium generation live.

A sensation culture

A strong case can be made out that the driving force behind contemporary culture is the desire for pleasurable sensation. Indeed, our very first description of culture as a 'culture of contentment' suggests exactly this point. For what are all the aspects of consumer culture we have already identified if not sensation-centred? Consumerism, science and technology, information technology, the media – all are driven by the demand for pleasure. Our entire culture is geared to this purpose.

The distinguished sociologist Zygmunt Bauman has provided a penetrating analysis of what this means. He argues that people no longer find their purpose and identity in producing things or serving others but in experiencing pleasures. The modern individual goes all out to achieve ever greater sensations and stimuli whether they be spending and shopping, alcohol, sex, sport, computer games or drugs. The typical individual in contemporary society organises his or her life around maximising pleasure and minimising everything that detracts from it. In Bauman's words, the individual's life is 'lived as the role of a *pleasures collector* – or, more exactly, a *sensations-gatherer.*'[7]

> **People no longer find their purpose and identity in producing things or serving others but in experiencing pleasures.**

Interestingly, Bauman cites the modern obsession with physical fitness as an example of this. In recent years, fitness has become a central purpose not as a necessary part of healthy development of body and mind (*mens sana in sano corpore*) but as an end in itself. Why? Because only fully fit people can experience sensations to the full. In the modern view, says Bauman, 'the body is first and foremost a receiver of *sensations*; it imbibes and digests *experiences*; the capacity of being stimulated renders it an instrument of *pleasure*. That capacity is called fitness…'[8]

But, of course, the story doesn't end there. A drawback appears. The demand for sensations and pleasures can never be fulfilled. No sooner is one peak reached than another looms into view: 'The body's capacity for vivid sensation and ecstasy is doomed to be forever short of the elusive ideal … impatience climbs the ceaselessly rising pile of successive disappointments, spurred by suspicion of inadequacy.'[9] Consequently, the relentless pursuit of pleasure is a wild goose chase. It can never be satisfied. The sensation culture is hollow.

As if in support of Bauman (though not knowingly), Mackay supplies the following comment from an Australian teenager:

> 'We hang out in parks and we drink. We go camping and we get smashed. We go swimming and we get smashed. We go to the drive-in and we get smashed. We go fishing and we get smashed… Being with each other and not doing anything that you have to do is fun. We go to the pub, talk about cars and get drunk. We are getting smashed basically nearly every night. In fact, I know some people who have been drunk every night since New Year, and we're into March already.'[10]

This is pretty crude stuff. Not every young person is so hooked on such unsubtle pleasures. But strip away the emphasis on alcohol and the message is one that fits contemporary culture well: pursuit of pleasure is the ultimate life-goal. And there's nothing wrong with it.

Two further examples, rather less drastic and somewhat nearer to the experience of children, illustrate how near at hand the values of the sensation culture lie.

The first is shopping. Once upon a time you shopped in order to live. Nowadays, the order is reversed: to live is to shop. It has become almost a hobby. A day at the shopping mall is seen as a leisure activity. It doesn't matter too much whether you buy anything: the pleasure lies in looking and fantasising. A new term has even crept into our vocabulary: 'retail therapy'. The young people portrayed in *Neighbours* use it regularly.

The second example is even more close to children's lives: the world of virtual reality.

Two-and-a-half miles from where this book was written, in the centre of Nottingham, England, stands a statue commemorating the greatest outlaw of all time, made famous by Errol Flynn, Kevin Costner and a host of lesser film and TV stars. Who do I mean? Why Robin Hood, of course.

One hundred yards further along the road, it's possible to enter a building and find yourself in the supposed world he inhabited. *The Robin Hood Experience* (as it's known) takes you back in time to Sherwood Forest, the Merry Men and, of course, the evil Sheriff of Nottingham. For a few pounds, it's possible to imagine you have been transported back into the Robin Hood myth (I say myth because it's questionable whether he even existed. And if he did, it certainly wasn't in the way the legend would have us believe).

This kind of experience is known as virtual reality. It can take many forms: a physical environment such as a theme park (Disneyworld is perhaps the best-known example), a computer game or even a computer-generated imaginary environment experienced directly by the brain through an electronic headset. Anyone who has seen the film *The Lawnmower Man* or is familiar with the concept of the holodeck in the *Star Trek* series will know what I mean.

It is now technologically possible to create an artificial environment that to all intents and purposes seems like the real thing, but which is not.

David Porter offers a definition that describes electronic virtual reality very well. It is: 'the creation of a world that appears real to the observer, with which he or she can interact, in which choices and actions made have real effect – but which exists only in the mind of the person experiencing it and the calculations of the programmer.'[11]

The point is that it is now technologically possible to create an artificial environment that to all intents and purposes seems like the real thing, but which is not. The advent of computer technology ranging from the personal computer to commercial computer systems that operate fairgrounds, theme parks and the like has meant that much more lifelike and apparently real situations can be simulated than ever before. As Porter notes: 'At the same time that the Internet has been expanding and changing our relationship to information and knowledge, the science of virtual reality has been escalating.'[12]

Virtual reality, especially through the medium of Playstation or Nintendo computer games is now an everyday occurrence for children. From a very early age, they are exposed to it.

The rapid growth of virtual reality technology has made it a common television experience. You can buy headsets which let you 'see' a virtual world. Sensors attached to your body and hand allow you to manipulate a virtual replica of yourself in the virtual landscape. You can go to entertainment arcades where two people stand in podiums a safe distance away from each other, wielding swords. They cannot see each other in real life. But in a virtual world they see each other's electronic self and can fight each other – even virtually 'kill' each other.'[13]

This is the reality (not the virtual reality) of the culture in which our children are growing up. What could better exemplify its insatiable demand for stimulus and sensation?

A morally confused culture

We've seen that the people of Clumber Street are a pretty tolerant lot. And in many ways, that's an attractive feature. None of us would wish to live in a street full of stiff-necked, self-righteous Pharisees continuously poking their noses in where they weren't wanted.

But behind the issue of tolerance, there lurks a much bigger question: how to agree on issues of right and wrong where conflicting viewpoints arise. If we were to go back four hundred years, the answer would be relatively straightforward: what did the Bible and the church say? Although people may have disagreed on specific moral issues, there would have been wide agreement about where to turn for authoritative guidance.

No such possibility exists nowadays, however. The days have long passed when the majority of people would regard Bible and church as authoritative in matters of morality. The rise of individualism (as we have noted) has meant that individuals are the final arbiters in deciding what is right and wrong.

So in Clumber Street we find an array of views and practices in relation to family life and sexual relationships. Each household organises itself as it wishes. Mike and Jo Tyler at number 1 lived together with their baby Tyler for a year before getting married; Rachel and James Symons at number 7 are a single-parent family; Barry McDonald and Sarah Wilson at number 9 are unmarried with children but live as if they are married; the three students at number 11 do their own thing individually, ranging from the conservative and quiet Brian to the hedonistic Zoe; the Watkinsons at number 13 are an amalgamation of two previous families (an increasingly common phenomenon); while at number 19, Linda and Ellen represent perhaps the most radical departure from what was once the norm.

But, of course, that's precisely the point: there is no longer such a thing as a norm. Twenty – even ten – years ago, a gay household contemplating adoption would have been regarded as way out, if not unacceptable. Now the residents of Clumber Street scarcely bat an eyelid.

The reason why no norm can be agreed is that contemporary Western culture lacks a source of shared moral authority. In morality, as in politics and economics, the right of the individual to choose is paramount. Provided such choices do not interfere with the choices of others and provided they do not wreck society, a wide disparity of beliefs and practices is acceptable. In a consumerist culture, pick 'n' mix morality is inevitable. And it's up to the individual to do the picking and mixing.

The effect of all this is to produce moral confusion among children and young people. Where everything is a matter of choice, it's inevitable that different individuals will make different choices, usually on the basis of what works for them. The Options generation has thus bequeathed to its children, the Millennium generation, not only a bewildering array of moral choices but – even more problematically – no coherent means of choosing between them.

Putting the Pieces Together

W e began with a bird's-eye view of an imaginary street in an imaginary town. This enabled us to identify a number of major features of contemporary culture.[14] But why is such an exercise important? Surely, children finding faith is a purely personal matter?

I hope that by now the reader will have grasped that children don't grow up on desert islands. From the moment they enter the world they are bombarded with sights, sounds, sensations and ways of thinking about the world that shape their growth and development in every way. Whilst they are individuals, they also take their cue from society. Their worldviews will to a large extent reflect the worldviews of the society in which they mature. We should never underestimate the extent to which we are all products of our age.

But having said this, I would want to stress also that children are capable (as are we all) of *transcending* their cultural context. They are *more than* products of the society in which they grow up. Theologically, we would want to say they are made in the image of God with all that implies.

Effective evangelism, then, will need to recognise both these truths. This is why the evangelist must understand something of the culture in which the gospel is proclaimed as well as understanding the gospel message itself. In years gone by, we have tended to stress the latter but ignore the former. I hope that by the end of this book even the most sceptical reader will appreciate that to hold such a view is no longer possible. Children find faith in their personal and cultural contexts: this is where God is at work.

Notes to chapter 1

1   Quoted in Francis Bridger and David Atkinson, *Counselling in Context,* London: Darton, Longman & Todd, 1998, p93.
2   Quoted in Bridger & Atkinson, p119.
3   Bridger & Atkinson, p119.
4   From Hugh Mackay, *Generations.* Reprinted by kind permission of Pan Macmillan Australia Pty Ltd. © Mackay Research Pty Ltd, 1997.
5   Mackay, p140.

6   Leslie J Francis & William K Kay, *Teenage Religion and Values,* Leominster, Gracewing 1994, p151.

7   Zygmunt Bauman, *Life in Fragments,* Oxford, Blackwell 1995, p.115.

8   Bauman, p116.

9   Bauman, p117.

10 Mackay, p137.

11 David Porter, *Children at Risk,* Eastbourne, Kingsway 1998, p177.

12 Porter, p177.

13 Porter, p177

14 The features I have described are sometimes known as postmodern. For a further overview, see David Lyon, *Postmodernity*, Buckingham, Open University Press, 1994.

2 The birth of faith

Babyhood: day one to twelve months

Lee

The first year of life is a whirlpool of experiences for baby Lee. He does not know it yet, but the basic patterns of his future are being formed in these early months. Most basic of all is the experience of simple trust, and it is from this that Lee will develop the capacity for faith. As with many things, this experience began at birth.

Like the rest of the human race, Lee will never consciously remember his birth but, tucked away in the depths of his subconscious, is the memory of that first experience of separation. For the first time, he was no longer physically tied to his mother, no longer surrounded by the warmth, comfort and protection of her womb, but now, instead, a separate being. At the moment of his birth Lee became distinct but dependent. In years to come, he will be told that when he curls up in a warm bed with his knees beneath his chin, he is unconsciously returning to the security of the womb. But for now, Lee knows nothing of that. At only a few weeks old, he instinctively turns to his mother for everything he needs, both physical and emotional. He may be separate from her but is not separated.

Fortunately, Lee's mother loves him dearly. He is not her first child and neither will he be the last. But he is to be her only son. She does not know this yet (which is just as well) and her love for him, although different from that which she lavished upon his older sisters, is no less free and generous. With only instinct to guide him, Lee has, in his first year, come to know the meaning of love and trust in the little world that fills the boundaries of his existence.

This trust has been directed towards *persons*. Or to be exact, one person – Lee's mother. Whenever he has needed her, she has been there.

Food, warmth, safety have all been found in her arms. As time has gone by, Lee has discovered that these things come regularly and reliably. Initially, he was fearful if he woke and his mother was not there. When first this happened, he experienced sheer terror. But he soon learned that his source of love was never far away. The constant experiences of touching and being touched, cuddling and being cuddled, holding onto and being held, have assured Lee that the world is orderly, kind and dependable. They have given Lee a far deeper understanding of love and trust than any later form of words will be able to.

Lee therefore knows what it means to have faith. To be sure, he doesn't have any idea what the words mean – words mean nothing to him yet – but he knows what it is to trust and to have that trust honoured. Lee has taken his first step of faith.

But there are other things Lee has been learning. For the first few months, the world to him was one sensation after another. He loved the colours, the shapes, the noise, the attention – they all captivated him. Everything was the world and the world was everything. And he was in the middle of it.

Slowly Lee came to distinguish one object from another. What he was later to call a pig was distinct from what he would discover to be a duck or a teddy.

And there was another thing. By the time he was nine months old, Lee had begun to realise that these objects could be hidden, and he wanted to search for them. Only a few months earlier, it had been a question of 'out of sight, out of mind'. If they were hidden, he just forgot about them. He had no image of them in his mind. But now, wonder of wonders, Teddy, Piggy and Ball and all the rest of them stuck in his head. If his mother removed them, Lee was soon to be found crawling around in search of them. The world had become a place of permanent objects, persons and places.

> **When he accidentally banged his hand against his highchair while in a tantrum, Lee soon learned that some patterns of behaviour were definitely not to be repeated!**

Throughout this period, Lee began to discover the use of his body. Within the continuous flow of sensations and objects he slowly started to distinguish different things and experiences. Lee also began to discover that he could react to and even influence them. He found out, for instance, that if he reached out for Teddy and flexed his fingers, he could hold Teddy's hand and pull him over. Bit by bit this action came to be repeated until Lee understood simple acts of co-ordination.

Not all was easy, though, and some actions brought pain. When he accidentally banged his hand against his highchair while in a tantrum, Lee soon learned that some patterns of behaviour were definitely not to be repeated!

... and Lizzie

Now let's turn to Elizabeth. Although born in the same ward as Lee, she is not destined to be so fortunate in her early months or years. For Lizzie (as she will come to be known) is not really wanted. She was an 'accident'. The youngest of a family of six, Lizzie's mum has had a lifetime of being last. But despite this, she soldiered on to gain some secretarial qualifications and left school to take up a decent job with a firm of computer manufacturers.

No sooner had she done so than she fell in love with a boy at work and within months moved in with him. The thought of starting a family could not have been further from her mind. But nature was to overrule and along came Lizzie within a year.

At eighteen, Lizzie's mother is furious and frustrated. Her career has ended before it has had a chance to begin and she sees herself as tied down for life. Although the baby is not to blame, Lizzie remains the ever-present symbol of the trap in which her mother is caught.

It is little surprise, then, that Lizzie receives none of the warmth and love lavished upon Lee. Not for her the constant affection shown by word and touch. Not even the regularity of feeding can overcome the intense rejection which her mother radiates towards her. From the beginning, baby Elizabeth experiences the most bitter feeling of all - that of not being wanted. As the years ripen, she will come to know the pain that only those who have been rejected from birth can know. In time, she will come to say for herself the words which have not been spoken by her mother but which do not need voicing for they silently fill the air: 'I wish Lizzie had never been born.'

In the meantime Lizzie, like Lee, learns the basic control of her limbs and the permanency of objects. But she does not know the permanency of parenthood. Her mum has left her boyfriend and they are now living as a single-parent family. What's more, she has found a way out of her dilemma: Lizzie is farmed out to a childminder while her mother resumes her career. In the first year of her life, she has no father and a mother who resents her.

Of course, it need not have been like this. But the reality is that Lizzie's relationship with her mum will always be blighted: it could succeed only if there were a genuine sharing of love, affection and trust. However, this will never be the case. As a result her sense of rejection will remain with her for years to come.

Within eighteen months of their births, then, we have two infants whose lives could not be more at variance: Lee who is loved and valued and Lizzie who is unloved and rejected. The one learns faith through the most fundamental of human experiences: the love and affection of the doting parent who sees her child as a gift and a treasure. The other knows nothing of faith for she does not know how (or whom) to trust in a world where adults seem only to care for themselves. When, in time, Lee and Lizzie come to hear of their heavenly parent who they will be told loves them like a father, their differing infant experiences of parenthood will, like a hidden, underground river, flow through their personalities to influence for good or ill their respective capacities for faith.

What is faith?

The stories of Lee and Lizzie are not uncommon. Although fictional, they are drawn from real life – from the observations and recollections of many hundreds of people compiled in the course of research into child development. We do not have to be researchers, however, to recognise the Lees and Lizzies of our lives. For most of us, Lee and Lizzie will ring true. For some who read this book, they will ring all too painfully.

The central point in this early infant period is that children unconsciously absorb attitudes of trust through their relationship with parents, particularly with their mother. The foundations of faith are being laid even at this early stage. A child who does not learn how to trust adults now will have difficulty trusting anybody at more than a superficial level later on.

This extends to trust in God. A valuable exercise in any congregation would be to find out how many adults who once made professions of faith in Christ and then dropped away had experienced disrupted patterns of trust in their early months or years.

> *The foundations of faith are being laid even at this early stage. A child who does not learn how to trust adults now will have difficulty trusting anybody at more than a superficial level later on.*

We should not be surprised if high proportions of children, and adults with emotional problems that go back to their childhood, find it difficult to stick with their initial commitment to Christ. Their desire to follow him may be completely genuine and they may long to love and be loved both by God and by Christian people. But, in the crucial first months of their lives, they have missed out on the fundamental experiences of trust-building. As a result they find it hard to trust and to believe that others trust them at the deep levels of their beings. Most of all, they cannot feel that God loves or trusts them. For if even those who brought them into the world do not accept them, why should God?

In this situation the minister, evangelist or friend has to realise that the vital stage of trust-building which was lost in infancy must now be made up for in the life of the child or adult convert. The rejection or lack of acceptance experienced during infancy has to be replaced by the experiencing of *constant*, patient love. This will not be a matter simply of words. The statement, 'We trust you, please trust us', however kindly meant, will not be enough, for the damage that has to be mended has taken place at a much deeper level. The hurt of that child or adult can only begin to be unlearned when they experience our continuous *acceptance* of whatever they can offer – no matter how irregular or incomplete this may be. In many ways, it is not the adult or older child who is acting and speaking to us at this point: it is the infant inside, who has never experienced acceptance and trust. The word of the Lord to us will therefore be, 'Be patient, be gentle even as I am patient and gentle.' It will not be, 'Castigate and threaten this sinner for backsliding.'

It is imperative, therefore, that we grasp the crucial importance of the first months of life and the spiritual effects of the relationships established during them. The capacity for faith is a wonderful but fragile thing.

Faith, however, is not dependent simply on human development. We are also forced back to *theological* questions: What is faith? How does the development of the capacity for trust relate to biblical teaching about what it means to have faith in God? We shall spend the rest of this chapter examining a theological understanding of faith in the light of what we have begun to see from the study of child development.

The gift of God

The story of Lee and Lizzie so far is the story of the human dimension of faith. But this does not invalidate or squeeze out the divine. Because God is creator as well as redeemer, the natural processes of human development are part of his ordering of the world. The human and divine aspects of faith are bound together like Siamese twins. So before we go on to look at how faith can develop throughout a person's life, we must establish a definition of faith which is true both to Christian theology and to how we develop as people.

The Bible makes it clear that faith is a gift of God. It cannot be won or earned – it is given by God (Philippians 1:29; 1 Corinthians 2:5). But how does this fit in with the idea of faith development, especially in the lives of children who may not be consciously aware of having received faith?

The answer lies in understanding faith as part of God's gift in creation as well as his gift in salvation. The two are intimately connected because God is the Lord of both, as the incarnation demonstrates. When, therefore, we think of children as somehow possessing faith 'naturally', we do not mean that they do so independently of God. He is the author of their lives from the beginning and it is by his grace in creation that they (and we) are capable of trust and of response both to other human beings and to God himself.

So faith is from start to finish a gift just as the whole of life is a gift. It does not begin at the moment we accept Christ as Saviour, though in the work of salvation God takes the faith he has given us as part of his creation and by grace transforms it into saving faith in his Son. By the transforming power of the Holy Spirit, saving faith arises out of the way God has made us in creation: it is all of a piece, the nature of which is wholly gift.

> When we think of children as somehow possessing faith 'naturally', we do not mean that they do so independently of God.

The capacity for faith that is given to us as God's creatures, however, is divinely planted but humanly exercised. Although it is given by God, it is nevertheless we who exercise it. James Fowler, the American writer on faith development, has proposed that we should understand this human exercise of faith as an activity which enables us to make sense of our lives. Faith, he says, is 'our way of finding coherence in and giving meaning to the multiple forces and relations that make up our lives.' Faith is thus 'a person's way of seeing him or herself in relation to others against a background of shared purpose and meaning'[1].

Fowler's definition has the advantage of treating faith seriously as a human activity, and provided it is understood in a theological context such as we have discussed, it is useful. However, we must insist that it is not the *activity* of faith alone that is decisive: equally important before God is its *content* or *object*. A Hindu, Buddhist, Moslem or humanist may all exercise faith in their different ways. But it is only through faith in the risen Christ that salvation may be found. The capacity for faith given at birth must lead to faith in Jesus for its fulfilment.

From an educationalist's perspective, Thomas H Groome has argued that Christian faith must be seen in three Christ-centred dimensions: faith as believing, faith as trusting and faith as doing.[2] To these we may add a fourth: faith as imagining. When all are present in the lives of Christians, they are exercising truly biblical faith.

To some, this last point may seem controversial. Surely, to see imagining as on a par with believing, trusting and doing is to lay too great a stress upon its importance? It may be seen as an adjunct to the others (so the argument might run) but not as an equal partner.

Such a view is understandable but, in my view, misplaced. As I shall argue below, imagination is crucial to faith because none of us has faith in abstract concepts in themselves but in the God who lies behind such concepts. And once we begin to think and talk about God we find ourselves imagining what he must be like. We conjure up all kinds of pictures in our minds to help us get to grips with the abstractions of theology. Images of an elderly gentleman on a cloud, a cosmic judge or even of a brilliant light abound in contemporary culture. They permeate people's conscious and unconscious thinking alike, both inside and outside the church.

Imagination is central, therefore, to faith. And when we come to read the Bible – say, the Gospels – our imaginations get to work with a vengeance. Even to read of the biblical world or to follow the stories of Jesus, requires active imagination. We cannot escape it. The challenge is not to let it have free rein but to ensure it is informed by truth. In this respect, believing and imagining are Siamese twins.

1. Faith as believing

It is a Sunday morning. The congregation is half-way through the weekly service of Holy Communion. The preacher has just finished his sermon and the vicar stands up to lead his flock in making their response to the word of God. At this point, the Anglican service (for example) is quite explicit about what form such a response should take: it should take the form of saying the Creed.

In this way, week by week, the equation of faith with the holding of theological propositions is reinforced. Even the most unintellectual believer cannot escape the conclusion that faith is first and foremost an act of the mind. 'I believe in … God ... Jesus ... the Holy Spirit ...' is almost invariably translated to mean 'I believe the following about God ... Jesus ... the Holy Spirit ...' This emphasis upon faith as an intellectual activity has frequently been overplayed. But the importance of believing in doctrinal truths should not be understated. Throughout history Christianity has claimed that being a Christian cannot be just a matter of feelings. There must be a core of beliefs which can be propositionally stated and which must be assented to if the believer is to be regarded as an authentic follower of Christ.

The reason for this is straightforward. The church in the first four centuries quickly and repeatedly found that all kinds of groups were ready to claim the authority of Christ for an assortment of views (many of them heretical), especially when it came to controversy about the person of Jesus. Time after time it became essential for the church to set out what it believed in order to sort out the doctrinal sheep from the goats. A glance at the history of heresies shows how necessary this process was. The same is true today with the growth and spread of cults such as Jehovah's Witnesses, Mormons, Moonies and the rise of the New Age movement. Without a clear idea of truths concerning God, Christ and the Spirit, Christians would be fair game for any sect which came along. As Groome has commented: 'The *activity* of Christian faith, therefore, requires in part a firm *conviction* about the truths proposed as essential beliefs of the Christian faith.'[3]

Historically, however, this emphasis on the role of the *mind* in the activity of faith came to present a major difficulty. By the time of the Reformation, the intellectual component of faith was regarded as the most important. The Reformers stressed afresh the importance of the heart and will in addition to the intellect, but in the late seventeenth century a new movement in secular philosophy began which came to elevate reason as supreme. This movement was known as the Enlightenment.

The Enlightenment swept over Christian Europe like a tidal wave. It proclaimed human reason as the supreme instrument of progress and the means by which individuals could be freed from superstition. (Christianity was held up as an example of such superstition.) Those who elevated reason above all else were consequently known as Rationalists – a term and a philosophy that has continued down to the present day.

The Christian church reacted to the Enlightenment in two ways. On one hand there were those who spurned reason in favour of reliance upon an inward work of the spirit, a kind of 'inner light' as the Quakers called it. This had the enormous advantage of bypassing reason altogether and thereby avoiding any need to confront the Rationalists on their own ground. When challenged about the intellectual validity or coherence of their faith, all the proponents of the inner light (or *illuminists* as they were known) had to do was to take refuge in an inward revelation from God or a direct experience of the spirit. They did not need to justify themselves in the court of reason: they merely had to say, 'The Lord has told me this and you cannot disprove it.'

The second Christian reaction of Rationalism was to assimilate it.

This was achieved usually by claiming that God had given reason as his divinely appointed instrument for understanding the world and his will. By itself, this claim was not incompatible with Christian faith. It is perfectly possible, and indeed important, to see reason as *one* of the means God has given us to understand his orderly and coherent creation and to discover his will. But the belief arose, and is still held today, that God could *only* be understood and related to by means of human Reason (with a capital R). Revelation quickly became squeezed out along with miracles. Neither of these could be accepted unless they could be squashed into a Rationalist mould. So the feeding of the five thousand was reinterpreted as an act of communal sharing, misunderstood by the Gospel writers; and miracles such as the calming of the storm were seen as the normal workings of nature dressed up to prove the divinity of the man Jesus.

> Unfortunately Christians all too often find themselves forced into a polarised choice between faith as intellectual assent and faith as inner emotional commitment.

It is hardly surprising that the English church of the eighteenth century came close to death and that only the combination of the Wesleyan, Evangelical and Anglo-Catholic revivals of the eighteenth and nineteenth centuries saved it from becoming merely Rationalism with a religious face.

What we face today, therefore, are the effects of this struggle. If we picture faith as a four-legged stool, believing the truth of theological propositions is one leg, but it is only one. Imagining, trusting and doing form the others; and all four are necessary. Unfortunately, owing to the impact of, and hangover from, the Enlightenment, Christians all too often find themselves forced into a polarised choice between faith as intellectual assent and faith as inner emotional commitment. In biblical terms it does not need to be like this: faith can be both belief about, and commitment to, the One who is both the Truth and the Lord of heart and minds.

2. Faith as imagining

One of the more malign effects of the Enlightenment preoccupation with reason was to squeeze out the role of imagination as an acceptable route to knowing and understanding. As science came increasingly to the fore, a contrast was drawn that has persisted down to the present day. On one hand there was the realm of so-called 'hard facts' which could be investigated by scientific experiment; on the other, there existed only subjective opinions, beliefs and prejudices which could not. Thus began the great divide in modern thinking by which only scientifically-verifiable information could be counted as trustworthy fact while everything else had to be regarded as mere personal opinion.

Imagination, of course, fell squarely into the second category. By definition, it is personal and subjective. It is not difficult, therefore, to see how the imagination came to be disparaged as inferior to the rigorous logic of science with its ruthless determination to root out anything that could not be proven as fact. In a world that values success in science and technology above all else, products of the imagination come a poor second. Imagination, as far as everyday life is concerned, is reckoned to be irrelevant to what really counts – the world of hard fact.

This is the climate in which generations of children have grown up. Little surprise, then, that they are encouraged in adolescence to 'progress' from imagination to reason as a necessary step towards so-called maturity. Imagination is seen as childish. It is assumed that as they move through adolescence, children will want to jettison it as they shed their childish ways and move onto adulthood. The 'real' world is concerned with being 'productive' and 'useful' as opposed to being an idle daydreamer. In the words of theological writer James Mackey, 'imagination is seen as ornamental and peripheral to the main business of life which is carried on by the sciences and in its practical form by technology, by the creation of wealth and the raising of material standards of living.'[4]

What should we make of all this? The most important thing to grasp is that this view of imagination is profoundly anti-Christian. From a theological perspective, imagination is not a childish irrelevance to be discarded in favour of allegedly 'adult' reason. Rather, it is a fundamental aspect of God at work in us, and as such, must be valued and encouraged rather than devalued and disparaged.

Theologically, therefore, we must affirm the role of imagination for two reasons: firstly, as the word implies, imagination is concerned with images. By using our imagination we can conjure up all kinds of mental images or pictures which either carry us into make-believe realities (as, for example, in science fiction) or help us to think about a reality we have never seen but of which we have heard (for example, a country we have never visited but can conjure up in our mind's eye). These are the ways in which we usually think of images and imagination.

We need to remind ourselves again and again that the image of God is not confined to our rational faculties but is to be seen when we creatively allow our imaginations to get to work.

When we use our imagination in this way for *creative* purposes (though not for self-centred or destructive ones), we are doing something very important: we are echoing the creative acts of our Creator God himself. Put another way, our creativity is a reflection of God's own creativity. And for this reason alone we should never despise the God-given instrument of imagination. To do so would be to deny one of His most precious gifts.

But there is a second reason we should take the imagination seriously. As far as we know, it is an attribute peculiar to humanity: other creatures simply do not possess it. The capacity to imagine is thus a feature of the image of God in us. It is part of what makes us, in the Psalmist's words, only 'a little lower than the heavenly beings' (Psalm 8:5). To quote the American theologian Harvey Cox, '… fantasy is the richest source of human creativity. Theologically speaking, it is the image of the creator God in man.'[5] Cheryl Forbes puts it like this: 'Imagination is the *imago dei* (image of God) in us. It marks us as God's human creatures. It helps us to know God, receive his grace, worship him and see life through his eyes.'[6]

In other words, when we use our imaginations, we are exercising God's image in us every bit as much as when we use our reason. In contrast both to the Enlightenment and to much of the church's history, we need to remind ourselves again and again that the image of God is not confined to our rational faculties but is to be seen when we creatively allow our imaginations to get to work. Reason and imagination together serve the glory of God.

But how does imagination work? What does it do? The following points have been identified:

Imagination is a way of seeing life. By using it, we are able to make sense of our lives and create meaning and purpose: 'All the information we receive about God, our responsibility as his stewards, our role as husbands, wives, sons, daughters, siblings, employers or employees is so much dust without imagination to help us act on the information.'[7]

Imagination transforms life. We all know how a boring day or humdrum chore can be transformed by a splash of imagination. Brother Lawrence used to imagine himself doing God's washing up as he washed dishes in the monastery. Some Christians use the opportunity of driving on a long journey to imagine Jesus sitting in the passenger seat. They then have an imaginary conversation with him – an imaginative way of praying indeed. But there is an even more profound point to be made. In Jesus we see a double image in the same person: the image of God and the image of humanity. The incarnation, in speaking of him as the God-Man, presents us, as it were, with a coin that has an image on both sides. When we look at one side we see the humanity of the man from Galilee; when we look at the other, we see the Godhead revealed.

The effect of this is to make us realise that God values us as human beings rather than as unembodied souls to be saved. By taking flesh, he demonstrated beyond doubt his love for humanity. And in the life – and death – of his Son, he revealed what it meant to be truly human. What's more, in Jesus' death, resurrection and ascension, he showed the pattern for a transformed humanity, no longer subject to the dictates of sin or imprisoned by death. The new humanity made possible by the cross and exemplified by the risen Christ, is a transformed humanity made possible by the Son who is at one and the same time the image of the invisible God and the forerunner of a transformed human race.

When we grasp the force of this truth, we begin to see the possibility of all kinds of transformations in our daily lives. Our *self-image* can be raised as we realise what it means to be precious to God ('if he has made me in his image and loves me I must be worth something after all'). Our *image of others* can change as we see the image of God in them and the ways in which he longs to make them more like the image of his Son. Our *image of the world* is challenged as we no longer see it merely as a playground for our pleasures or as a place of despair – we picture it instead as God's world created, redeemed and loved by Christ. Our *image of the church* as a bunch of misfits and hypocrites is transformed by a vision of it as the body of Christ and the family of God. In short, by faith we re-image (or re-imagine) the whole of life as the creative, image-remaking power of God moves within us.

Imagination opens windows onto another reality. We have noted how, in everyday life, imagination enables us to construct alternative realities, to daydream of imaginary worlds. C S Lewis's Narnia and Tolkien's Middle Earth are two well-known literary examples of this. So are the universes of *Star Trek* and *Star Wars*. But there is yet another reality (not fictional this time, but historical) into which we can gain entry by means of our imaginations – the biblical world revealed to us in scripture. Here there exists a vast array of stories, characters and truths upon which our imaginations can get to work. The liberating power of creative imagina-tion taking us back into the reality of biblical events can, time and time again, bring us to a fresh encounter with Christ in the here and now. The combination of imagination and scripture is a powerful one which evan-gelical Christians (including me) have frequently overlooked for fear of getting into unsubstantiated fantasy that can so easily lead to heresy. But it need not be like that. Under God, our imaginations – when devoted to his glory and informed by scripture – can open up the riches of his grace in ways not possible through the use of reason alone. Imagination and faith go hand in hand. And, as in so many things, children can show us the way.

3. Faith as trusting

Consider the following statements:

  (a) 'Good morning Mr Jones. I trust that you are well today.'

  (b) 'Trust and obey, for there's no other way to be happy in Jesus, but to trust and obey.'

Both contain the word 'trust' but there is a difference: (a) represents faith in a state of affairs. We trust *that* poor old Mr Jones is not under the weather. In (b), however, we are exhorted to trust *in* a person – Jesus. Being happy is tied to a personal relationship of faith and obedience.

Of course, the two may be brought together when we trust that a state of affairs is satisfactory because we have faith in the person responsible for them: 'I trust you will find this cake to your taste, Vicar. My wife baked it this morning and you can always trust her to turn out a winner.'

When we speak of faith in God as 'trusting', we have in mind this combined meaning. We not only trust what God says or does, more fundamentally we trust *him* as a person. As we reflect on this, we begin to move away from a purely intellectual and propositional definition of faith. Christian believing becomes more than assent to a series of statements about God: it moves into the area of personal relationship.

James Fowler has helpfully characterised this as *covenantal faith*. A covenant is an agreement or bond between two persons. Both parties are pledged to each other and there is a flow of trust in both directions. Each has faith in the other that what he promises will be fulfilled. Covenantal faith is thus rooted in relationships which are trustworthy and dependable.

The example *par excellence* favoured by the biblical writers was the covenant between God and Abraham. (Note that the partners in a covenantal relationship do not have to be equals. It is enough that they engage in a bond based on mutual trust.) Between Genesis chapters 12 and 17 (supplemented by Paul in Romans 4), we read that God took the initiative in re-establishing a covenant with Abraham and that Abraham responded in faith.

This covenant involved two-way trust. On Abraham's side, he had to believe God's promise that despite his age and the barrenness of his wife Sarah, Abraham would become the father of many nations. Moreover, he had to trust when God commanded him to leave his home and travel to Canaan where he had no kin, no wealth and no security. The trust God demanded could not have been greater: 'Leave your country, your people and your father's household ...' (Genesis 12:1). How many of us today would listen to a sudden command from an unknown God to do away with all our familiar security, and travel abroad where we are promised blessings impossible by any natural standard?

Yet, as Paul says, 'Against all hope, Abraham in hope believed and so became the father of many nations, just as it had been said to him...'

(Romans 4:18). Covenantal faith won for him blessing and righteousness. God, for his part, trusted Abraham. Abraham's shady dealings with his wife in Egypt make it clear that he was as humanly frail and fearful as the rest of us. Yet the fact is that Abraham persevered and in faith reached the promised land. The trust God placed in him was fulfilled.

But the story of Abraham illustrates a crucial aspect of covenantal faith in God. Paul reminds us that despite the natural odds against the fulfilment of God's promise to him, Abraham 'did not waver through unbelief regarding the promise of God, but *was strengthened in his faith* and gave glory to God' (Romans 4:20; italics mine). In his weakness, Abraham found that far from being abandoned by God, God built up his faith and thereby cemented the covenantal relationship. Abraham was not left on his own to fail. The exercise of trust within the divine covenant is thus wholly a matter of grace. We are back to the notion of faith as a gift. The covenant between God and humanity serves as a model for all forms of covenantal faith. It contains the characteristics essential to a bond between persons: it is personal, mutual and gracious. A healthy parent-offspring relationship will exhibit all these in the first months of life. As we have seen, it is here that the human source of faith is to be found.

4. Faith as doing

Luther described the letter of James as 'an epistle of straw'. He believed its emphasis upon good works undermined the Reformation recovery of Pauline teaching on grace and faith. For Luther, surrounded by the corrupt philosophy of salvation by works which had come to characterise the medieval church, the rediscovery of grace and faith brought liberation and hope.

But however right Luther may have been in his context, we cannot ignore the fact that for the New Testament writers, faith and works were inseparable. The mere profession of faith in God must be backed up by evidence of a new way of life – the life of the kingdom. 'Not everyone who says to me "Lord, Lord," will enter the kingdom of heaven, but only he who does the will of my Father who is in heaven' (Matthew 7:21). Likewise, Paul's great teaching on salvation by faith in the first eleven chapters of Romans is followed immediately by four chapters of practical instruction as to what it means to live out salvation in behaviour and relationships.

Faith, then, is not a matter of feeling right before God. It is grateful acceptance of the gift of redemption, and a readiness to do all that follows from it. It is a matter of saying, 'I am saved by the mercy of God. Now what must I do to live out the new life that is within me?' James 2:14–17 has the answer:

'What good is it, my brothers, if a man claims to have faith but has no deeds? Can such faith save him? Suppose a brother or sister is without clothes and daily food. If one of you says, "Go, I wish you well; keep warm and well fed," but does nothing about his physical needs, what good is it? In the same way, faith by itself, if it is not accompanied by action, is dead.'

It is an unfortunate side effect of the reaction against Rationalism and the retreat into a feelings-based faith, that much modern Christianity has failed to take this biblical command seriously. Such has been the fear either of lapsing into salvation by works or of falling into a dependence upon human reason, that we have neglected the 'doing' aspect of faith.

Of course, it is fatally easy to substitute a works-centred religiosity for a living faith in the free grace of God. But the antidote for this is not to avoid the 'doing' aspect of faith but to understand that our relationship with God through Christ requires us to be doers of the word and not hearers only (James 1:22). If we are to be truly biblical in our discipleship we have no choice.

Faith, then, contains these four dimensions: believing, imagining, trusting and doing. If the task of the evangelist is to present the gospel so that people may *come* to faith, then we must recognise that evangelistic strategy has to be geared up to enabling individuals to *grow* in it. Evangelism which concentrates on only one dimension to the exclusion or minimising of the others is untrue to its name and untrue to God.

Conclusion

It is clear that of these four dimensions of faith, the third – trusting – is the key to relating faith to young infants. The categories of believing, imagining and doing are aspects which must await a later stage of development beyond the experiences of babyhood.

This helps us to understand the importance of the early months, up to one and a half or two years. As we have observed, it is in this period that the 'trusting' leg of the faith stool is formed. When we later come to speak of God as our heavenly Father and we encourage children (or adults for that matter) to trust him, it will be to the deep wells of infant trust that we shall be calling. For children like Lee, our appeal is likely to find an echoing response. They will at least know what it means to have experienced trust, acceptance and love at the hands of a parent. For children like Lizzie, however, the likelihood is much less. That is not to say that the Lizzies of this world are incapable of responding to the gospel: by the grace of God they are. But the kind of response they make and the emotional soil out of which it arises may be very thin indeed. We should not be surprised to find a response based on a desire to please or to be accepted by the adults. The nature of trust in these circumstances will be fragile and precarious and we shall need to be as wise as serpents and as harmless as doves in seeking to strengthen it.

In the light of all this, is there any evangelism that is appropriate to young infants? The answer, perhaps surprisingly, is 'yes'. But it will consist entirely of a relationship of love. It will contain no intellectual message nor will it call for a response other than to trust in the human who shows love. It will be a gospel of cuddles, smiles and softly spoken words. These are the seeds out of which, by the grace of God, fuller faith may develop.

Notes to chapter 2

1   James Fowler, *Stages of Faith*, New York, Harper & Row 1981, p4.

2   Thomas H Groome, *Christian Religious Education*, New York, Harper & Row 1980, p57

3   Groome, as above.

4   James Mackey, *Religious Imagination,* Edinburgh University Press, 1986, p3.

5   Quoted in Leland Ryken, *Triumphs of the Imagination: Literature in Christian Perspective*, Downers Grove, IVP 1979, p97.

6   Cheryl Forbes, *Imagination: Embracing a Theology of Wonder,* Bromley, Marc Europe 1986, p18.

7   Forbes, as above.

3 The growth of faith

Infancy: thirteen months to six years

Lee's confidence

Babyhood gave way to infancy. With this came a torrent of new experiences – like the time when Lee spoke his first word. He was about fifteen months old. Predictably enough the word had been 'Dada'. But what struck Lee's parents was the way he then called every other man 'Dada'. Lee could simply not distinguish. he just thought that all men were called 'Dada'.

Communication

It was not always to be the case. As Lee grew more fluent in using words (he did not always understand their meanings) he discovered a much greater power over his world. He could command and control the objects around him. He could tell his parents what he wanted. He could be precise about where it hurt when he felt ill. And, above all, he could communicate with his friends. Language was the gateway to society and his place in it.

Independence

Then there was the other great occasion of independence – Lee's first unaided walk. It was not very far; but it was enough to set him on the road to mobility and autonomy. By four or five he had completely mastered the control of his limbs. Lee had begun to establish himself as an independent person in his own right.

Playgroup came – and went. Lee enjoyed every moment of it and there he took another step forward in understanding. For the first time, he came to realise that the world consisted of more than his own family. It slowly dawned on him that he could no longer get away with many of the things he had done at home. The playgroup leaders were not so easily manipulated as his mother and his sisters. Lee learned, the hard way, that a tantrum would not be rewarded with a biscuit and a glass of milk but with some stern (although loving) words while other children got on happily with their finger painting. He was going to have to take account of others.

Of course, Lee *tried* to get his own way. The world might now be larger than that of his infancy and he might no longer be at its centre all the time; but he could still act as if he were.

Identity and will

This theory was put to the test in the summer of the year Lee went to playgroup. By then, Lee had established for himself a sense of identity and will. It even extended to Ted, his favourite bear. The two of them would sit down together each afternoon to discuss the day at playgroup and other important matters such as what they might have for tea. But it was not until the day before the trip to the seaside that Lee's parents realised quite how strong their son's identity had become.

It had all begun with a conversation about what they should take on the outing. Lee insisted that he should take his tricycle. Dad pointed out that there wouldn't be room in the car; Lee was sure there would be. And so it went on. After a short time, tempers were rising on both sides. Lee was determined the trike should go and Dad was determined it shouldn't. Needless to say, as with many such exchanges, Dad imposed his authority and it all ended in tears and an early bedtime. The tricycle did not go the next day but Lee's parents were careful to note their son's independence of spirit and wisely took it into account in future.

Lee's next great experience was school. He quickly settled and gained a reputation as 'a strong-minded and determined little boy', a comment occasioned by Lee's insistence after two days that he could make his own way to the toilet, thank you very much. (Fortunately it was next to his classroom.)

Stories

It was in the year before starting school, and during his first year there, that Lee developed a love for stories. Although he used to enjoy watching television, his love for hearing stories was just as great. Through story books at home and at school, he entered enchanted worlds of magic, excitement and adventure. He heard about pigs and wicked wolves, little old ladies who lived in vinegar bottles, witches and wizards, fairy princes and princesses. His imagination took off.

No less important at this time, however, was Lee's growing sense of awe, wonder and beauty. As his powers of imagination grew, so did his capacity for these. Without realising it, he was beginning to develop the capacity to reach towards God.

Lee also heard about Jesus.

To Lee all these stories were rolled into one. At first he got them mixed up so much that he couldn't quite remember whether the pigs lived in a vinegar bottle or which house the witch had magicked into rubble. And where was it that Jesus and God lived? Oh yes, it was in the forest near the little people, wasn't it?

Slowly, Lee began to get the stories sorted out in his mind. But even by the time he went to junior school, he still wasn't sure what kind of magic Jesus had used to feed all those people and heal the sick men and women. And what was all this about Jesus and God living up in the sky? Mum and Dad had flown up in the sky when they went to visit Aunty Jane in Australia. Had they seen Jesus on the way? They must have done, Lee supposed, but neither of them had said so.

Little by little, the building blocks of Lee's personality were being put into place. It would be some years before the construction would be anything like complete, but the shape of the building was becoming clear. It might be redesigned or built upon further, but it would never be dismantled.

Lizzie's unhappiness

Humiliation

If Lee had a happy infancy, however, Lizzie suffered the opposite. Her mother came to like or love her no more as time passed. It didn't help that the childminding service was arranged on a rota so that from one day to the next Lizzie never had the same adult to relate to. To make it harder, she was sometimes left with a reluctant aunt who didn't want Lizzie any more than her mother. It was here that Lizzie experienced her first humiliation.

The occasion was little more than a minor inconvenience, Lizzie soiled herself by accident (she was three). Her aunt was extremely angry, smacked her and sent her to bed for the rest of the afternoon. From that moment on, Lizzie became fastidious in toilet matters. She also lived in fear and trembling of her aunt and would even pretend illness rather than be left there for the day.

By the age of four, then, Lizzie had not found a single adult to whom she could entrust herself freely and totally. It seemed that the adult world, far from offering security, reassurance and confidence, presented only rejection, humiliation and anxiety.

Play

Things changed with the advent of playgroup. Lizzie's mother was a bit late in getting her into this but the nine months she spent there were the best of her life. For the first time she mixed with other children of her own age. There were interesting things to do and there were *toys*.

Now Lizzie had never been allowed many toys. In fact, her mother frowned upon play as something wasteful and useless. Lizzie's main stimulus had been the television. But at playgroup a whole new world opened up to her. She would spend hours just going from toy to toy, playing for a time with each one in turn. Dolls, bears, donkeys, ponies, telephones, tricycles, houses – they were all sheer joy. The end of each day was a heartbreak. Would she be allowed to see them all again?

Alternative lives

It was during this time that Lizzie met the first adult who seemed interested in her. This was the mother of another girl at playgroup, Wendy. Unlike Lizzie, Wendy was not an only child; she had a brother two years older and a sister one year younger. She and Lizzie became friends.

One day Wendy invited Lizzie home for tea. Lizzie's mum was only too glad, so the two little girls, escorted by Wendy's mother, excitedly set out for Wendy's home.

Lizzie's time there was better than she had ever known before. There were delicious things for tea and Wendy's mum and dad showed a kindness she had never met. Lizzie had no way of knowing whether this was always the case but she was happy enough to accept the kindness of the moment. But what struck her most of all was an incident involving Wendy's brother Colin. It was quite unlike anything Lizzie had experienced before.

> *She came to see that punishment could be combined with fairness and love; that it did not have to be a matter of capricious and unpredictable rage and that she and her friends might not be such hopelessly bad people after all.*

Colin was a very active boy. He was always running about, shouting and making himself known to whoever would listen. People usually did listen for he had a way of winning you over even against your better judgment. But Colin did not like playing with girls, least of all his younger sister. So when Wendy came home with another girl, he decided to make his attitude clear. The result was a spider down Wendy's neck (he did nothing to Lizzie) which produced howls of terror and rage.

This, startling though it was, was not the thing which most left its mark on Lizzie: it was the way Colin's mum dealt with him. To be sure, Colin got a severe telling off and lost the right to watch television for three days; but there was no sense of rejection in the punishment. Once the matter was dealt with, it was regarded as finished. The errant boy was accepted once more. Wendy kept her distance from him for a time, but that was a precaution as much as a sulk. As Lizzie came to know Wendy's family better, she came to see that punishment could be combined with fairness and love; that it did not have to be a matter of capricious and unpredictable rage and that she and her friends might not be such hopelessly bad people after all.

Had she known it, Lizzie was beginning to acquire positive images of herself, of parenthood and family life, and was beginning to learn the meaning of trust.

Confusion

By the end of her first year at school, Lizzie was living in four worlds:

(a) home which she dreaded and disliked; (b) school, which she liked but in which she was not very confident; (c) Wendy's which she loved and wished she could live in all the time; and (d) the inner world of fantasy and imagination, which she fell into when she wanted to escape from the realities of home. Like Lee, Lizzie revelled in stories. But unlike Lee, she used them as daydreams to distract her from whatever might be going on at that time. More and more, she found her teacher recalling her from some magic world where all grown-ups were kind (except for the wicked witch) and children could play for ever. By her seventh birthday (by which time she, too, had moved up to a junior school), Lizzie was truly mixed up.

Patterns of faith development

Whathat patterns of faith development can we discern within the life stories of Lee and Lizzie so far? How should these affect our attitude to children's ministry?

Capacity for trust

Emotionally, we continue to see the importance of the parent in the formation of a child's capacity for trust. The love and attention which had surrounded Lee from his birth continued through his infancy. Adults were neither a threat nor a source of fear for him, as they were for Lizzie. They offered acceptance, confidence and affection.

This proved crucial in Lee's development as an independent personality. By late infancy he had become aware that the world was not simply a matter of himself and his desires: it comprised other 'selves' who also had *their* lives and desires. The love of his family enabled him to begin to establish *his* identity in its own right without fear that he would be humiliated or squashed.

We continue to see the importance of the parent in the formation of a child's capacity for trust.

For Lizzie, life told a different story. Her early rejection at the hands of all the adults who mattered, and who were responsible for her, instilled in her a deep mistrust of the adult world. The adults who dominated her infant world either failed or refused to accept her, while the constantly changing rota of uninterested carers was bound to produce an acute sense of worthlessness. Had Lizzie heard about the love of God, or about the notion of God as her heavenly Father, it is unlikely that emotionally she would have been able to respond in any but a negative way.

Relating outside the family

It is in the infant stage, however, that children begin to learn to relate to others outside the family. This introduces an entirely new set of considerations. No longer is reality confined to the narrow range of people who have surrounded the child from birth. He or she must now come to terms with wider society. For both Lee and Lizzie, the playgroup provided the bridge into a social environment not centred solely on the family. But whereas Lee was ready to co-operate (albeit to a limited extent) with other children, Lizzie needed to make up for the many practical deprivations of her early years. Having been deprived of toys and play facilities she desperately needed to feel free among such things in her new setting of playschool. Consequently, her capacity and readiness for making relationships was limited. Even more than most children of that age, she was still turned in upon herself. (This is a characteristic of all infants up to about seven but is accentuated in those like Lizzie.)

We noticed, too, the formation of identity in this stage. Lee's tussle with his parents about the trip to the seaside represented not so much a streak of stubborn naughtiness (however much it seemed that way to the adults) as an assertion of independent personhood. This is crucial if the development of a mature capacity for choice and judgment is ever to take place. Children who become content to rely on the judgment of others or upon the consensus of their peers have failed to develop a fully independent identity. This frequently has its roots in infancy. In adult years, even among Christians, this can lead to shallow faith, which under pressure, is unable to stand.

Significant, too, is the combination of firmness with fairness. Wendy's mother knew this in her punishment of Colin. But the reason it impressed Lizzie was that she had known only treatment that was arbitrary and rejecting. The idea of punishment operating within a framework of justice and love was unknown to her. Again, this will have implications for her understanding of, and reaction to, Christian teaching about God, Jesus and salvation.

These factors contribute to the setting into which knowledge of Jesus will arrive. They constitute the soil in which the seeds of the gospel will be planted. But what kind of seeds are appropriate for children moving through this stage?

The gospel and children's capacities

Story

T he most important fact is that whatever the *content* of Christian teaching may be, its most fruitful *form* will be that of the story. We have seen how both Lee and Lizzie lap up the medium of story. It is *the* way in which children of this age learn. We must recognise, too, that the child at this stage of development finds it hard to disentangle one kind of story from another. Jesus, God and fairies are all of a piece. They all inhabit the same world. There is no difference between miracles and magic.

This presents the evangelist or children's worker with a problem: to use miracle stories or not? One possible conclusion might be that at this stage of development the use of miracle stories runs the risk of being misleading. Because they are not yet capable of distinguishing between magic and the miraculous, the danger is that children will inevitably confuse the two and Jesus will be seen as another kind of wizard or magician. No amount of telling the child that Jesus is not really magical will make any difference. The child's framework of understanding and interpretation will still most likely put miracles in the category of magic. Even if we successfully get children to say it is not so, they will still be prone to confuse the two. We might as well get them to recite Einstein's Theory of Relativity.

But such a conclusion may be too drastic. Roger and Gertrude Gobbel in their book *The Bible: A Child's Playground* make the point that as adults we need to refrain from imposing or expecting an adult interpretation of scripture from children. We must allow them to enter the biblical stories on terms that make sense to them as children and not on terms created and imposed by adults determined to force them into a specifically adult way of thinking. If children see the miracles of Jesus as magic, it doesn't matter (at least not initially) because this provides an entry point into scripture by which children will engage with the Jesus of the Gospels, even if they interpret what he does through childlike eyes. As adults we have to accept this and encourage it if we want children to interpret the Bible for themselves. We shall return to this theme in the next chapter.

> ## As adults we need to refrain from imposing or expecting an adult interpretation of scripture from children.

There is, however, one important proviso to this. As children grow older, they can gradually distinguish between what the significant adults in their lives believe to be true and what they see as 'make-believe'. A child whose parents do believe in miracles, and who are able to make a distinction for the child between magic and the power of God, is much more likely to develop a healthier view of miracles than a child whose parents disbelieve or have not got beyond the magical stage themselves. This underlines what we have noted earlier, namely that the *context* of teaching is the key to a child's understanding.

Understanding in terms of experience

A second aspect of a child's capacity in this period is the way in which everything is interpreted in terms of his or her day to day experiences. Carol Mumford records the response of one six-year-old to the wonder of the sun. Note how the child understands the new experience only in terms of what he has already experienced:

> I think it's marvellous that the sun stays up in the sky. I think some string is holding it up. Why doesn't it fall down?[1]

Or the five-year-old who watched her mother get dinner ready one day and asked what God has for his dinner. The conversation which followed went like this:

Mum: God doesn't have any dinner.

Mary: Well if he doesn't have any dinner, does he have an egg for his tea?

Mum: (*wondering how to explain*) God doesn't have any tea either, dear. He doesn't need to eat because he hasn't got a body.

Mary: (*having pondered on this*) I see what you mean. His legs come right up to his neck.[2]

The implication is not simply that we should avoid using figurative language about God but that invariably children will form an image of God based on their own experience of the world around them. Information drawn from scripture or from the adult's experience will be translated by children into terms which make sense within their life world or within the mental world they have constructed from stories, television and other sources. Even where the *words* (such as 'God') are identical with adult vocabulary, the images and meanings attached to them will be different. As Violet Madge observes: 'Young children will attempt to integrate whatever comes into their experience into a meaningful pattern, be it angels and magnets, sun and rocks, seeds and babies, aeroplanes and heaven, God and shops, Jesus and baby-sitters.'

Unconnected logic

Thirdly (this is related to the previous point), we need to realise that just as children at this stage of the developmental sequence possess a particular emotional and psychological structure, so they also possess a corresponding *logical* structure. The most characteristic features of the way children reason in this stage are fluidity and apparent unconnectedness. Different bits of children's thinking pop up in a seemingly unrelated fashion. It is all a jumble. To the adult mind, their statements often contain no logical coherence and there is no connection between them. God gets mixed in with all sorts of natural and historical events in random fashion. Faith developmentalist James Fowler gives a good example of this. In his book *Stages of Faith* he records a conversation held with six-year-old Freddy about what a family might see deep in the woods. It illustrates well the points we have been making:[3]

Freddy: They see - you can see deers, you can get sunshine. You see beautiful trees. You see lakes and you see clear streams.

Interviewer: Well tell me, how did all of these trees and animals and lakes get there?

Freddy: By rain – Mothers get the babies. The sun shines through the clouds and that's a lot of fun. Yeah, the stream and the water lakes. The lakes – the lakes get um, more – the forest – you have a deep hole and then it rains and then when it's full enough they – it's a – it's a lake. But when it gets stinky you can't swim.

Interviewer: Oh I see. Well why do you think we have trees and animals?

Freddy: 'cause God made them.

Interviewer: I see. Why do you think he made them?

Freddy: 'cause, 'cause there's two reasons why. Number one is 'cause trees give off oxygen and number two is 'cause animals protect other animals.

Interviewer: I see, I see. Well why are there people?

Freddy: Uh – I don't know.

Interviewer: Can you think what it would be like if there weren't any people?

Freddy: The beautiful world would become ugly.

Interviewer: How come?

Freddy: 'cause nobody would be down and the world would be ugly.

Interviewer: Yeah?

Freddy: I think it would be like in the old days and things.

Interviewer: And what was it like in the old days?

Freddy: Like there was big hold-ups. There was wagons going fast.

Interviewer: But what – what about even before that? What if there weren't any people anywhere?

Freddy: Just animals? I think it would be like – be like an animal world.

Interviewer: Would that be good?

Freddy: No, if there weren't any people, who would be the animals?

> *Interviewer*: Well, how did people get here?
> *Freddy*: They – they got here from God? That's all I know
> about the old days.

This interview reveals clearly how 'unadult' a child's logical system actually is. Freddy jumps from one point to another, answering the questions by drawing on what he has seen on television or heard in stories. His descriptions of the old days is a blatant example of this: hold-ups and wagons. Likewise, his concept of animals seems to be that they are rather like humans inside animal skins: 'if there weren't any people, who would be the animals?' he asks. Perhaps we see here shades of the Disney culture.

The child in late infancy therefore has images of God which are extremely confused. Given that the child constructs his understanding of God from everyday experience, we should not be surprised if such images are crudely human:

> *Interviewer*: Can you tell me what God looks like?
> *Freddy*: He has a light shirt on, he has brown hair, he has
> brown eyelashes.
> *Interviewer*: (*looking at two statues of Christ*) Does
> everybody think God looks like that?
> *Freddy*: Mmm ... not when he gets a haircut.[4]

Capacity for play

Children love to play. Like imagination, play is fundamental to a child's world. Yet, as with imagination, adults disparage it. 'Stop playing and listen!' hisses the mother to her fidgety son in church. 'Okay, playtime's over. Let's get back to work,' commands the teacher at school. For adults, the real world is concerned with productive, goal-directed tasks. For children, reality is defined, to a significant extent, by play. Joan Cass writes: 'Play is as necessary and important to a child as the food he eats, for it is the very breath of life to him, the reason for his existence and the assurance of immortality.'[5]

Why is play important?

There have been many theories of play, all of which offer complementary insights into its nature and importance to children's growth and development:

- According to the nineteenth century poet Schiller and the philosopher Spenser, play is the product of surplus energy. The active, growing child must 'let off steam', and play is the vehicle for doing so. On this account, play is definitely a childish thing. Adults either have no surplus energy or it is directed into productive tasks.

- By the start of the twentieth century, a more scientific explanation had developed. Karl Groos, studying the play of humans and animals, argued that play arises out of an inborn instinct for survival. Children learn interpersonal, social and fighting skills which ensure survival in later years. At the instinctual level, they are preparing themselves to survive in a competitive adult world.

- The early 1900s also saw the rise of Freud's theory of play: that it represents an attempt to come to terms with the failure to satisfy desires and drives which have been denied. The boy who acts out a game of cowboys and Indians, for example, is channelling the urge to be violent into a socially-acceptable game. He cannot actually go around killing people, so he does so in a world of make-believe. The girl who plays with dolls is acting out the instinctual drive to motherhood.

- Linked to this is the view that play is a kind of catharsis, a way of purging feelings of anger, aggression and so on. It also represents a child's attempt to master or control feelings previously regarded as frightening or overwhelming by giving them an outlet in an acceptable and controlled activity. Aggressive sports are perhaps an example of this.

- One influential view of play, is that of the educationalist Jean Piaget who argued that children's play fulfilled two purposes. The first, he called *accommodation*. Here children attempt to come to terms with experience by accommodating themselves to the external world and interacting with it through playful activities. A baby grabbing a rattle or pushing a mobile seeks to gain some kind of mastery over her environment by literally laying hold of it. She accommodates herself to it. The second purpose Piaget called *assimilation*. In this, the child uses play to show how much she has assimilated the world around her, how much she has absorbed experience she has observed and made it part of herself. Make-believe play such as nurses and doctors, or pretending to be mummies and daddies is a good example of the assimilative process at work to enable a child to integrate information and experience.

- To these, we must add a completely different view: that play, especially fantasy play, is an exploration of alternative ways of making sense of the world. On this view, play is not so much educational as emotional, reflective and imaginative. It touches the parts other approaches don't reach. It is a way of entering into other worlds of meaning in order to check out and open up the 'regular' world. Through its use of the imagination, this kind of play enables us to explore and express emotions, to act out and resolve disturbing aspects of life, to achieve desires and ambitions beyond the scope of ordinary life and to create new worlds of meaning. A life lived in this playful world can allow us to integrate those aspects of 'real' life that without fantasy would remain unexplored and unresolved. It is a form of play that is immensely powerful and occupies a prominent position in children's lives. We should never underestimate or belittle it.

Yet none of these theories quite captures two essential theological truths: firstly, that like imagination, play is a reflection of divine creativity. When children play, they are expressing something of the image of God in them, in addition to the functions suggested by the theories above. If this is true, we need to recognise that play is a pointer to God, a reminder that he is present even in the most basic of children's activities.

> *Play enables us to explore and express emotions, to act out and resolve disturbing aspects of life, to achieve desires and ambitions beyond the scope of ordinary life and to create new worlds of meaning.*

But, secondly, if children use imagination and fantasy play to create worlds of meaning where difficulties are faced and resolved and where everything turns out alright in the end, there exists an area of ministry for which the gospel is explicitly designed. Not in the sense of providing another fantasy but of offering a truthful story of how God has acted to make things right. As Mary Collins puts it: '...children aspire to construct a world where despite pain and danger things turn out alright after all. This hope for a world more real than the world they live in creates in the human heart a readiness to hear the Good News.'[6]

Conclusion

Round about the age of seven, the average child reaches a boundary. He or she begins to move from infancy to juniorhood. This is marked publicly by the transition from infant to junior school. A new phase is assumed to have begun. There is no turning back.

But life-long patterns of personality have been established. As we have seen, the first stages of child and child-faith development are characterised by the impact of personal relationships. It is these, particularly between a child and its parents, which are crucial in the formation of identity, outlook on the world, and the capacity for covenantal faith.

However we look at it, there are considerable implications in all this for evangelism and ministry to children. We need to be aware that almost everything we say will be reinterpreted according to what children already know by experience or have had passed down to them (which is a form of experience). But what effect will this have upon the content of our message? We shall close this chapter with some suggestions for teaching children at this stage of development.

On the cautious side, we shall:
- be careful about how we teach miracle stories, though we shall not necessarily rule them out. Nothing sounds more magical than the story of Daniel in the lions' den or the feeding of the 5,000 and although we should not be overly worried if children start their journey of understanding in this way, we shall want to be careful. If we decide to use miracle stories we shall think carefully about how to present them.

- avoid teaching material which requires adult modes of thinking or logic. This means finding appropriate ways to express abstract concepts such as sin, salvation, or redemption. It is difficult to recast these in infant terms, even if plenty of illustrations are used.

- be careful in our use of parables. As with miracles, their story form makes them attractive to children. But at a deeper level they are subtle and we shall need to be wise in choosing them. However, we need not be too worried: the important thing is that parables may provide an accessible way for children to begin their adventures into the world of the Bible.

● think twice about using religious fables in which animals are invested with human or divine characteristics. This can be confusing and lead to theological hang-ups at a later stage. If God is associated with the mythical in this way, he may be rejected when the child comes to reject all myths as mere make-believe.

Positively, however, we shall:
● show acceptance of a child, however difficult he or she may be. This does not mean we shall avoid reproving him or her, but we shall try to act like Wendy's mum – in love as well as justice.

● build on images and relationships of trust which have made up children's experience. If they associate the Christian worker with a warm and trusting relationship, they will be more ready to trust God.

● not worry if the content of our message says little about Christ as Saviour. It is faith defined as trust rather than knowledge that carries meaning for the child at this stage of development.

● focus on teaching which is easily understood in terms of a child's everyday world. This will probably centre on relationships and simple experiences of nature. (So, for example: God loves us like Mummy. God makes the trees grow.)

● construct teaching programmes which centre on stories of people and personal relationships. Stories about Jesus will be chosen to illustrate his love for people and children.

● teach in stories. This will require skilful storytelling which captures children's imaginations. Becoming familiar with story books written for four to six-year-olds will be helpful here.

● look for responses appropriate to the age and stage of development of each child.

To sum up, then. While it would be a mistake to think of the early years of childhood as no different from later years, it would be equally wrong to assume that there is no form of evangelism appropriate to this period. As the chart below shows, there is a direct connection between a child's formative experiences of relational love and his or her subsequent capacity for spiritual understanding and growth. The evangelist or children's worker does not need to be a Billy Graham but that does not mean he or she has no role.

The relationship between experience and belief

A relationship of shared trust, love and care

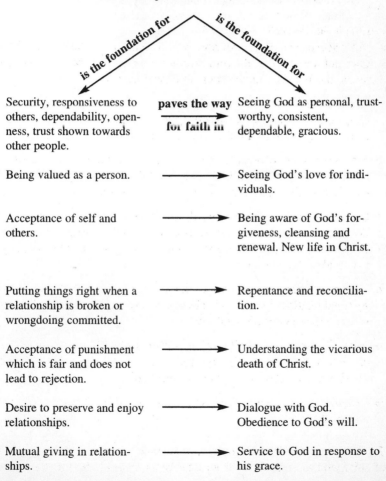

is the foundation for   *is the foundation for*

Security, responsiveness to others, dependability, openness, trust shown towards other people.	**paves the way for faith in** →	Seeing God as personal, trustworthy, consistent, dependable, gracious.
Being valued as a person.	→	Seeing God's love for individuals.
Acceptance of self and others.	→	Being aware of God's forgiveness, cleansing and renewal. New life in Christ.
Putting things right when a relationship is broken or wrongdoing committed.	→	Repentance and reconciliation.
Acceptance of punishment which is fair and does not lead to rejection.	→	Understanding the vicarious death of Christ.
Desire to preserve and enjoy relationships.	→	Dialogue with God. Obedience to God's will.
Mutual giving in relationships.	→	Service to God in response to his grace.

Notes to chapter 3

1   Carol Mumford, *Young Children and Religion*, London, Edward Arnold 1982, p35. Reproduced by kind permission of Hodder & Stoughton Ltd.
2   Mumford, as above, p60.
3   James Fowler, *Stages of Faith,* New York: Harper & Row 1981, p124.
4   Fowler, as above, p127.
5   Joan Cass, *The Significance of Children's Play,* London, Batsford 1971, p11.
6   Mary Collins, 'Is the Adult Church Ready for Liturgy with Young Christians?', in Diane Apostolos-Cappadona (ed), *The Sacred Play of Children,* New York, Seabury Press 1983, p7.

4 The blossoming of faith

The junior years: seven to ten

Characteristics of the junior

The junior school child is a wonder to behold. For Lee and Lizzie, juniorhood was a period of amazing growth in every conceivable way. Little more than enlarged infants when they entered the school, they emerged some four years later, well on the way to adolescence.

Increasing understanding

In common with their friends, they simply gobbled up information during this time. Lee once spent all day ploughing through *The Guinness Book of Records* 'just because I'm interested' (as he had remarked to his surprised mother). He also joined the local library and could be seen, regularly each Saturday morning, borrowing three or four books which he duly read in the course of the next week. He was not particularly studious – he simply liked finding out things.

Lizzie was equally curious (particularly about little-known facts) but she did not read much. Her favourite medium was television. Although she watched all sorts of programmes ('It keeps her quiet,' was her mother's reaction), it was not just a question of cartoons and soaps. She also watched *Blue Peter* and even children's news programmes because they contained lots of interesting information and human interest stories. She would never have read *The Guinness Book of Records* but she did watch its TV equivalent, *Recordbreakers*. To her surprise, she found that she and Lee knew the same facts.

This thirst for knowledge was accompanied by other developments. Shortly before the Christmas following her seventh birthday, Lizzie had been challenged by Colin, Wendy's older brother, about Santa Claus.

'Surely you don't *still* believe in Santa Claus,' he had crowed, 'I gave up that kids' stuff ages ago!' (In reality, it had only been 18 months.) At the time, Lizzie had been shocked: she had always believed in Santa Claus because that's what adults had always said. Now here was Colin saying the opposite! Whom should she believe?

Lizzie asked Wendy's mum who encouraged her not to worry too much about Colin: 'He loves to tease, you know,' was her reply. And that was that. Or was it? Needless to say, Santa Claus went the same way for Lizzie as he had for Colin, and by the time she was eight, Lizzie had come to learn that the fairy tale world of her early childhood was not the reality she had once believed. She still enjoyed the richness of fantasy stories, but that is what they now were – make-believe which excited and thrilled the imagination but which firmly belonged inside the head: they were not part of the 'real' world.

Knowledge, then, for Lizzie and Lee took the form of 'real' knowledge about the 'real' world you could see, touch and handle. If it wasn't 'real' in this sense, it wasn't true.

Knowledge for Lizzie and Lee took the form of 'real' knowledge about the 'real' world you could see, touch and handle. If it wasn't 'real' in this sense, it wasn't true.

This was reinforced by the way their reasoning powers were developing. By Year 6, both children had become interested in science. It was here that you could perform simple experiments and that was fun. But it was much more than that. Experiments enabled Lee, Lizzie and their contemporaries to understand the idea of cause and effect.

From then on, the notion of cause and effect became firmly embedded in their understanding. This was especially true for Lizzie. She could see that it was a fundamental principle of how the world functioned. Until then she had just accepted that things happened: now she began to look for the causes. Her logic had taken a leap forward. In her teenage years, this belief in the necessity of cause and effect was to make her highly sceptical of anything whose cause could not be demonstrated. And in the midst of the inevitable adolescent identity crisis, it made her full of self-doubt. For if, as she had come to sense strongly, her mother had never really wanted her, could Lizzie herself be the cause of her mother's rejection? But all that lay in the future: for the time being she simply absorbed the notion of cause and effect into her expanding world of knowledge and experience.

Lee and Lizzie had moved on from seeing the world in terms of disconnected events to thinking in sequence. If you ever asked them to explain what they had done that day, the answer always went something like: 'We did this, then we did that, then we both went off and did something else, then we came back again and then we watched TV, then we had something to eat, then we went out to play and after that we called on Wendy and Colin ...'

We all know this kind of conversation. It can take hours. But the fact is that for children such as Lizzie and Lee, the junior age is one in which the world ceases to be a jumble of unrelated events remembered at random and becomes instead a narrative world in which experiences are made sense of by recounting them in copious detail in the order in which they happened. Anyone who has listened to a summary of a film by a child of this age will know that it requires a great deal of patience on the part of the listener. (It can also help if you have already seen the film!)

So whenever Lee's mum asked him what kind of day he had had at school, she always got a very full answer, beginning with who did what to whom in the playground before school, and ending with details of the story his teacher had told at the end of the afternoon.

Lizzie did not tell her mum very much because she never asked.

Empathy and justice

One story had a particular effect on Lee. It was 11 November and his teacher had told a story of a young man of only seventeen years old who had been killed rescuing a wounded comrade in the First World War. It had made even more of an impact on Lee because the young man had been an Australian, and Lee's cousin lived in Australia. (Lee even kept in touch with him by e-mail and the family hoped one day to visit 'Oz' which everyone told them was a wonderful country.) The story had touched Lee deeply not so much because of the excitement and thrill of a war story – there hadn't really been any of that in the way the teacher had told it. It was more a question of empathy. Lee found himself imagining what it must have felt like on the battlefield, frightened but hearing the cries of a wounded friend. Then the dash into 'no man's land' to try and drag him back to the trench, followed by the sense of relief when the man was back – but then the fatal shot! And what must it have been like to die thousands of miles away from home in the mud of a strange battlefield?

It was not just that Lee could *imagine* the story: it was more than that. He could begin to feel as the heroic soldier had felt. He could begin to *identify* with him.

Although, of course, he didn't realise it, Lee was exhibiting a capacity which becomes increasingly noticeable in the junior child – the ability to see things from another person's perspective. Lee felt for the soldier because he could take the dead man's perspective. He could imagine the feelings of fear, loyalty and love for a friend which the man had experienced. He could begin to share something of the terror of the Australian youngster as he realised he was dying. In a particularly poignant way, the story brought out what was latent in Lee as in other children of his age and development – the ability to empathise.

Prior to this, as we have seen, infant and early junior children view events from an egocentric standpoint. They see the world out of their own self-centredness. To say this is not to pass a moral judgment: it is to describe the way young children function. They are literally not capable of taking a wider perspective. The world still centres on them as individuals and they can see it in no other terms. With the intellectual and emotional development of juniorhood, this expands into the capacity for empathy which in later years will, if developed, blossom into a sense of justice.

Despite the intellectual, emotional and psychological changes in this period, what stands out is that in their way of understanding, both Lee and Lizzie, irrespective of intelligence, remain rooted in 'concreteness'. This does not mean that they have stood in a bucket of cement, but that they do not yet think in abstract concepts. They still look at matters in terms of the everyday, concrete experience.

This was brought home to Lizzie's student teacher one day during Lizzie's third year. The teacher had been speaking of the injustices of the world. 'Injustice is a terrible thing,' she told the class. 'We must all fight to get rid of it.'

This rallying call, which would have been fine addressed to a teenager, unfortunately meant nothing to these ten year olds, as was evident from the silence when the teacher asked for examples. There was embarrassment as child after child said nothing, or passed with the words 'Don't know'. In the end, Lizzie piped up: 'You mean like children in Africa who get a leg blown off by landmines when they're just out playing in the fields, Miss?' Lizzie had remembered pictures of how Princess Diana had championed the abolition of landmines and in a few words had captured everything the student had meant but had been unable to communicate to the class. What Lizzie had done was to translate the abstract concept of justice into concrete terms intelligible to her classmates. Most of them were still stuck in the literal, concrete stage. There was no guarantee Lizzie could repeat her triumph but the point had been made and her student teacher was careful not to talk in abstractions again.

New loyalties

Another area in which both Lee and Lizzie (Wendy, too, for that matter) changed considerably in these years was that of group relationships. At infant school, the typical pattern had been for each child to act solely as an individual, even when part of a group. Team games, such as they were, had consisted not so much of a closely-bound team plying for team success as a collection of individuals playing as if they were in it only for personal enjoyment. The notion of group loyalty and commitment was non-existent. In the middle of a game, the infant child would just as likely wander off on their own as get ready to play for the team.

As the junior years passed this changed. Although still an individual, each child learned to act as part of a group. At play-time, they would go around in groups, each with its own identity. On games afternoons, woe betide the player who let the team down! After school, the older children would play out in the street in gangs. The practice of isolated individualism slowly gave way to social co-operation and peer group identity.

An incident in class one day demonstrated this very clearly. Lee's table had been slow in clearing up after art. As the time for lunch approached, Lee spilt a jar of water all over the floor and over another girl Vicki's dress. Vicki hit him and a fight broke out. The teacher, who had been at the other side of the room when it all began, rushed back to find a girl with a soaking dress and a boy with a heavily scratched arm. Vicki's nails had drawn blood. This was no mere 'whoops-a-daisy' incident.

No amount of questioning could make the group tell who had been involved. So they all stayed in as a punishment throughout lunchtime and again the next day. Both Lee and Vicki were grateful for the loyalty of the group and would have done the same in return. But what was striking was the way in which nobody gave them away: to have done so would have been regarded as 'sneaking' and would have forfeited the trust and acceptance of the group.

Such a situation would have been unthinkable five years earlier. No infant would have kept quiet about the culprits. Neither would he or she have been rejected as a sneak for telling the facts. But by year 5 at junior school, the notion of group co-operation and solidarity had become all-powerful. The self-centred world of the infant and early junior had been replaced by the social world of the later junior, with its network of group obligations and codes.

As we have seen, the junior years bring enormous changes in the intellectual, emotional and social development of a child.

Intellectually, we have noticed:
- a thirst for knowledge and information.
- a realisation of cause and effect.
- a redefinition of what counts as 'real'.
- an adjustment of infant make-believe.
- a recognition of the difference between reality and fantasy.
- an ordering of events in coherent narrative form.
- the predominance of literal and concrete ways of understanding.

Emotionally, we can see:
- a growing capacity to take the perspective of others.
- a sensitivity towards the feelings of others.
- a reduction in seeing oneself at the centre of the world.

Socially, the child increasingly:
- finds identity in groups of other children.
- learns to work and play as part of a group.
- develops an overriding loyalty to the group.

The effect on faith development

What effect will these changes have upon a child's development of faith? How do they relate to evangelism? It is time to return to three of the aspects of our four-fold definition of faith: believing, trusting and doing. (I have discussed the nature of imagination and the related concept of play in some detail in the previous two chapters.)

1. Believing

In the infant phase, the believing dimension of faith is barely visible. But the rapid growth in the desire and capacity for absorbing knowledge in the junior phase means that the intellectual component of faith becomes much more prominent. Children's natural curiosity about the world in general extends to religion, especially if they are confronted with believing adults or other children. They will want to know *what* their friends believe, though they may not yet be bothered about the *why*.

The content of Christian belief, however, may pose a major problem. One one hand, as we have noted, children in the junior years are fascinated by story. This gives the Christian evangelist or teacher a head start, as the gospel is the story of God's involvement with humanity. But on the other hand, children are now able to sort out factual stories from fantasy. Into which category will they put the Gospels?

> Unless the adults or peers whom children respect believe in the authenticity of scripture, the children will increasingly come to perceive the Gospel stories, especially the miracles and the resurrection, as mythical.

The answer will not be straightforward. It will almost certainly vary from child to child. But the chances are that unless the adults or peers whom children respect believe in the authenticity of scripture, the children in question will increasingly come to perceive the Gospel stories, especially the miracles and the resurrection, as mythical. A more sophisticated child may say that the Gospel writers got it wrong in their recording of events. But in an age such as our own, where the notion of *revelation* is meaningless to most people, it is more likely that the Bible will simply be written off or ignored.

We should not be surprised at this. After all, the definition of what counts as 'real' for the junior child turns heavily upon what can be observed and experienced by the senses. Junior children faced by stories of Jesus healing blind men, calming the elements, and eventually rising from death, are therefore faced with a massive difficulty – do they believe these things actually happened or not? This question is increasingly pressing as children grow older. What's more, the task is not made easier by the absence of such miracles from everyday life. But the conflict is heightened even further, if on one hand the storyteller himself clearly believes in these events, but on the other hand most of the world clearly does not. This puts to the test in a particularly sharp way children's acceptance of the authority and wisdom of adults. In the first half of juniorhood, the authority of the adult is still likely to win. Adults are still presumed to know everything and their word is accepted as true. But as children reach eleven or so, this intrinsic authority diminishes. 'Oh, that's only what Mr X or Miss Y believes,' becomes the reaction of the older child. The implication is that there are now areas in which the content of what even a respected adult says must be sifted.

Miracles and fantasy

One way in which many children (and adults too!) cope is by a process of compartmentalisation: Christian belief is consigned to a specific place or time, such as church or Sunday school, or it is put into a separate mental compartment which is sealed off from all the others. For example, children may happily accept the 'scientific' assumption that miracles do not happen and cannot happen and yet, at the same time, carry on believing that in the time of Jesus they did. Here, they have relegated miracles to history where they are safe from scientific scepticism. No one can travel back in time to check, and so we can give the Gospels the benefit of the doubt. This enables us both to have our miraculous cake and eat it. Theologies which hold that miracles ceased after New Testament times, of course, serve to reinforce this view.

> One way in which many children (and adults too!) cope is by a process of compartmentalisation: Christian belief is consigned to a specific place or time, or it is put into a separate mental compartment.

Or, children may simply live as if life is divided into separate worlds in which it is appropriate to believe different things according to whichever world they happen to be moving in at any given moment. So the world of church and Sunday school becomes the place where believing in miracles and Jesus goes on. But when it comes to school or play, no such belief is necessary. Life is divided into boxes, each of which has its own set of rules or beliefs. Provided they do not overlap, it does not matter if they are inconsistent with one another. There is no need for a *coherent* view of reality: what matters is that each compartment is consistent within itself and that the whole process works.

It may seem, then, that evangelists frequently find themselves faced with a choice. They can either carry on with miracle stories regardless of what educationalists are saying or shift the emphasis of their message away from the miraculous.

If they follow the first course, they may justify it by saying that the work of the Spirit in bringing children to faith makes it unnecessary to pay attention to theories of child development. But this would be both theologically and practically naive. The processes by which children grow and develop are well-established; and, as Christians, we would maintain that this is how God, in his wisdom, has structured child development. The evangelist or teacher who refuses to recognise and respect this is like a gardener who refuses to test the soil and then sows plants which cannot grow. When they die he or she does not question the method but simply blames the soil or the plants instead. Christian workers who refuse to take account of the multiple ways in which children develop need to ask themselves whether they are any wiser than such a gardener.

However, if they follow the second course, shifting the emphasis of the message away from the miraculous, they run the risk of ignoring crucial aspects of miracles altogether. This was the erroneous path taken by such academics as Ronald Goldman in the 1960s. It is perhaps more important, consequently, that evangelists should be clear about what they *do* wish to emphasise in the ministry of Jesus. Significantly, the Gospels record him as sparing in his use of miracles and make it clear that he did not use them primarily in order to impress his audience or convince them of his divinity or power. Instead, he used them out of compassion for suffering individuals and as signs to point to God's active purpose in the world in establishing his kingdom.

> We can try to evoke for children the sense of astonishment and wonder felt by the original observers.

This brings us to the nub of the problem. Given the likelihood that children will always tend to see miracle stories in terms of magic, can we use them creatively? I believe we can without abandoning their supernatural flavour. In the first place, we can try to evoke for children the sense of astonishment and wonder felt by the original observers. There is a proper sense of awe that the stories convey provided they are recounted sensitively. And awe is an important part of experience that leads to God. We are mistaken if we suppose that children who, after all are highly imaginative, are unable to glimpse something of the awesomeness of Jesus' actions. To be sure, some will interpret them as magic; but this can become the first step on their journey of faith rather than an obstacle in the way of it. The limited perception of Jesus as some kind of magician can give way to a true understanding. We should not therefore ignore miracles altogether or reduce them merely to charitable acts.

That said, the stories do convey the message that the same Christ who performed these marvellous acts is the Jesus who today calls us to be his friends. This gives us scope for a larger interpretation than the purely amazing nature of the miracles themselves. The addition of such a focus moves the hearer away from concentration on the 'magical' aspect of the miracles to what, after all, is the core of the gospel message: that God acts out of gracious love to meet the needs of sinful, suffering humanity. In this, the cross and the resurrection are the greatest miracles of all.

By emphasising Jesus' miracles as acts of love as well as awesome deeds, evangelists and teachers are thus able to speak openly and with integrity about the reality of miracles without overly-encouraging children's preoccupation with the magical. They can recount the Gospel stories without reducing them to mere acts of wizardry. Moreover, they can speak of them as historical events with confidence since they represent specific occasions on which God demonstrated how much he loved ordinary human beings who otherwise were helpless, and did so by breaking into the natural order of events.

Used wisely, then, the miracle stories of the New Testament can enlarge a child's understanding of Jesus. Taken together, both emphases – on awe and on love – present a rounded picture of what Jesus was doing. Used unwisely, however, they may simply reinforce notions of magic, which, in later years, will be discarded as infantile along with stories of pumpkins turning into stagecoaches and frogs into princes. It is a matter of sensitivity and balance.

If miracles pose a problem for children's sense of fantasy, the abstract nature of Christian teaching poses problems for their sense of literalness. The junior child thinks in concrete, literal terms. This requires us rigorously to examine our teaching in two areas.

Firstly, *we must be aware of children's tendency to use metaphorical language literally.* Phrases such as 'Take Jesus into your heart', or 'Jesus is knocking at the door of your heart', may conjure up pictures of him actually opening a little door inside our bodies. Likewise, talk of Jesus 'living inside us' will be equally misleading. I have heard children ask, after an evangelistic message based on this kind of language, in exactly which part of the human body Jesus makes his home.

It is a salutary exercise to spend time going through an evangelistic talk in advance, checking out the metaphors that are in danger of being taken literally. Remember, a child up to about ten and a half or eleven will interpret words literally that older children will grasp as metaphorical. Here are some examples:

The metaphor:	Could be taken to mean:	So should be rephrased:
Let Jesus into your heart.	Open up your chest.	Let Jesus be in charge of your life.
Taste and see the Lord is good.	God can be eaten like food.	When we know God as a friend, we will discover how wonderful he is.
You must be born again.	You must get back into your mother's tummy.	(See below.)

How great a danger is this, however? In the first edition of *Children Finding Faith* I argued that we should avoid figurative language wherever possible. But I now find myself persuaded that metaphor is an important tool by which children interpret the world around them and that although confusion is often the case, they are much more adept at handling metaphor than adults give them credit for. Moreover, metaphor is crucial in opening up the imagination; and since this is central to the faith process, it follows that we should be prepared to take risks with metaphor. While I would still urge us to think carefully about the metaphors we use, at the same time I recognise that the apparent confusion between figurative and literal may be the very thing that triggers an imaginative leap or a curious question from the thoughtful child. 'Mummy, I can't get back into your tummy, so how can I be born again?' may be exactly the kind of response that carries the inquiring Lee or Lizzie further along the journey into faith. So my advice now about the use of metaphor? Stay cool!

Secondly, *we must work at turning abstract concepts into concrete teaching.* The notions of sin and redemption, for example, presuppose an essentially adult ability to comprehend abstract truth. The only remedy for this is to translate the ideas behind them into *examples* which are intelligible to the literalistic mind.

This is not just a matter of using shorter words. Nothing could be shorter than the word 'sin'. But the term creates enormous confusion even among adults. It is far better to speak of 'doing wrong things', which is familiar and denotes a recognisable experience.[1] In this way the idea is retained without the abstract language.

The most concrete experiences for children are those which involve day-to-day relationships. To cast the gospel in terms of relationship, therefore, cashes in on the most powerful experiences in a child's life. It also, as we have seen, chimes with a growing awareness of the perspective of other people. To portray sin as the breaking of friendship with God and the death of Jesus as God's way of restoring that friendship can evoke powerful feelings as a child puts himself in the place of God the Father or of his Son.

Our purpose must not be to manipulate children's emotions but to enable them to get inside the skin of the gospel. A skilful presentation in terms which encourage the child to imagine how Jesus or his Father felt when faced with human sin will go much further than simply laying out the 'ABC' of evangelism or the 'four steps to salvation'.

We must work at turning abstract concepts into concrete teaching.

Believing at the junior age, then, is a very complex business. The evangelist who does not recognise the developmental characteristics of the phase will end up with one of two results: (a) children committing themselves to a message they have not understood, because they want to please; or (b) children who seem to accept what is said but whose capacity for future scepticism has been significantly increased.

2. Trusting

We have seen that trusting is the foremost feature of faith in infancy. Although this is overtaken by intellectual belief during the junior years, the patterns of covenantal trust established in infancy continue to provide the emotional framework for faith.

So it is that Lee can cope more readily than Lizzie with the intellectual challenges of the junior years because he is more secure when faced with the new knowledge that threatens his previous understanding. He is also more able to trust the adults who impart such knowledge.

For Lizzie, however, the absence of a love bond between herself and her mother from babyhood onwards makes it more difficult for her to handle new information or new ways of looking at things. It is much harder to launch out into uncharted waters if no one has ever taught you to swim or if you have never been able to trust anyone to do so. This is Lizzie's position when her previously uncritical ideas about Jesus and his Father come under threat from her classmates or from her own discovery of the material world of cause and effect.

Faced with this crisis, Lizzie can do several things: she can continue to believe in her infant-based notions of God, so that the developments in her general intellectual capacities are cut off from the area of faith; she can give up her previous beliefs completely; she can substitute faith in a person (probably an adult such as Wendy's mum) for faith in God. Or she can muddle along with a mixture of all three as she goes through the same developmental struggle and growth as other children. There is no way of predicting exactly which course the Lizzies of this world will follow; we can only be aware of the problems and possibilities.

For example, if she separates her intellectual capacities from her infant-based notion of God, Lizzie might simply lap up all we say, even at the late junior stage, when we would expect her to be asking more critical questions. Or, if she substitutes faith in the evangelist for faith in God, she may sidestep the challenge of our message ('Oh yes, I believe all that.') in order to fawn upon the evangelist in unswerving obedience and loyalty. Alternatively she may, for the same reason, make an overt and apparently enthusiastic commitment. Or she may be totally unable to make any emotional commitment at all since this would involve an act of trust that is beyond her capability.

Of course, not every child who exhibits one or other of these features is a Lizzie. All children are like this to some degree. But we do well to remember that children's reactions to evangelistic teaching are notoriously easy to misread. The evangelist who gets a hundred hands raised in response to an appeal will need to discern with care and wisdom what kind of processes have been at work. For it is very difficult to trust an invisible God at an age when the real world is defined as what can be seen, felt, touched, smelled and spoken to. Indeed, it is hard to know what is going on in a junior child who professes to trust in Christ. While we must not rule out the possibility of a work of faith similar to that experienced by adults, we must recognise that a more complex process is almost certainly at work – a process which will involve, on the child's part, an element of faith in the evangelist or teacher. He or she, after all, is the visible, tangible representative of the invisible Christ. And, moreover, the evangelist can enter into a face-to-face relationship with the child in a way that is impossible for Christ who is present in the world through his Spirit. Given the literalness and concreteness of children's thinking, it would be surprising if this element were not large.

The evangelist who gets a hundred hands raised in response to an appeal will need to discern with care and wisdom what kind of processes have been at work.

In saying all this, however, we need constantly to remember that faith in Jesus Christ is never only an outcome of human process. All people, whether children or adults, come to faith in Christ because God's Spirit is at work bringing them into a living relationship with him. The Spirit 'goes ahead', opening hearts, minds and wills to Jesus, so that faith is always and everywhere the result of God at work as he touches our lives even though we may not be aware of it.

3. Doing

The junior child is unbelievably *active* and eager to please. Many a parent will have reached the point of exhaustion while their children are still going strong, showing no sign of tiring. A child's understanding of faith as doing, is, therefore, a natural extension of this characteristic. Again, because of the concreteness of understanding at this age, children tend not to draw a distinction between faith and works. Doing is bound up with believing and imagining and cannot be otherwise.

Perhaps in this they are more biblical than adults. By perceiving faith in Jesus as a relationship, children automatically assume that this involves doing things. The notion of a faith which is purely reflective and which does not issue in activity is literally inconceivable. Although it might be possible to have activity without faith, the converse could not be true. You might as well try to imagine water that isn't wet.

So the evangelist who majors on 'learning by doing' is making a choice which is not only educationally, but theologically, sound. The evangelist or Sunday school teacher who expects passive absorption of ideas by a crowd of docile youngsters will get neither passivity nor absorption. This is especially important to remember in using story as a teaching medium for it is often perceived as passive. In fact, good story-telling is highly active. It will involve both the teller and the hearers through their emotions, imagination and, in some cases, the acting out of parts of the story itself.

Yet it is surprising how many people still believe that the most effective form of communication remains the set piece talk. This is a complete misapprehension. While the talk may achieve something if it forms part of a total package with plenty of activities, the talk itself will, in terms of learning, achieve only a limited amount. It is an established fact that children take in:

10% of what they hear
50% of what they see
60% of what they say
90% of what they do.

The implication is clear: communication and learning must be active and imaginative: as much about relationship as information.

The shift in focus

If faith during infancy is a matter of trusting with instinctive feelings, faith in juniorhood is a matter of believing with the developing intellect. (It is also concerned with the imagination, as we have seen.) With the junior phase, we have majored on the educational characteristics of the child since it is in this area that great strides are made. No less important, however, is that the focus of a child's existence shifts away from the relatively narrow boundaries of home to the expanding horizons of the wider world. School is especially important in this broadening process as the child becomes less and less dependent upon parents and family for knowledge, and more and more dependent upon teachers and classmates.

> *The evangelist who majors on 'learning by doing' is making a choice which is not only educationally, but theologically, sound.*

It is at school that the child is exposed to a cluster of differing or even conflicting beliefs which challenge the world in which he has grown up. In contemporary society, Christianity is simply one among many views in the marketplace of belief. The evangelist can no longer presume prior Christian understanding or knowledge of even a rudimentary kind. Although the term 'secularisation' is unthinkingly and often inaccurately used to describe what has happened in Britain over the last thirty-five years, it is nevertheless true that Christianity must now fight as hard as any other set of beliefs to gain a hearing or to win adherents, as our trip in chapter 1 to Clumber Street indicated.

This hotchpotch of beliefs makes it imperative that evangelists and children's workers understand the mental, emotional and social world in which our children operate. An appreciation of the process of child development during the crucial junior years is therefore especially important.

Taking spiritual stock

Experienced faith

It is now time to take stock of the spiritual side of Lee's and Lizzie's development. The infant and junior years belong to what John Westerhoff (mentioned earlier) has called the period of experienced faith.[2] It is the time when patterns of believing, imagining, trusting and doing are the product of what is learned from others. This may take the form of negative as well as positive learning; but it is learning nonetheless. In this, as we have seen and will see, the models provided by home, school, media and community are crucial.

In contemporary Western societies, Westerhoff's period of 'experienced faith' will be closer to Fowler's definition of faith as a system of meanings, than to a biblically-oriented Christianity. For reasons we have explored in chapter 1, the process of secularisation has entrenched itself so that it is now plausible to speak of the West as *post*-Christian.

So what might the evangelist expect to find in the 'experienced faith' outlook of Lee or Lizzie?

In neither Lee's nor Lizzie's case was Christian faith a significant factor in the outlook of their parents. Christianity was not important in enabling them to give meaning to their lives. They did not consciously draw upon it as a way of making sense of the world. If it had any relevance at all, it was in the realm of morality: 'do good to others, love your neighbour'. But even here it was rarely more than an unattainable ideal.

Relationships in the home

What was equally significant, however, for the development of Lee's and Lizzie's experience was the quality of relationships and values experienced by them in their early years. This gave a context for the system of beliefs which their parents held.

In Lizzie's case, the experience of rejection formed the bedrock of how she came to understand herself, her family and her world. Only with the advent of Wendy and her family did this begin to erode, as an alternative value – love – was shown. For Lee, love was part and parcel of life from the beginning. His understanding of himself and the world, therefore, was much better adjusted.

In teenage years, this could prove decisive. It is here that the struggle to find identity rages. A child like Lizzie who has experienced a lone-parent upbringing with little parental love will find it hard to believe in a God who is Father and who claims to love us as his children. It will not be much good saying to Lizzie, 'God loves you as much as your parents love you', for she has no experience of a fatherly relationship and a poor experience of relating to her mother. If Lee, on the other hand, is to come to faith in Christ at all, it will be the security of his relationship with his parents which, on the human side, paves the way. For Lizzie, her best hope lies in her substitute relationship with Wendy's parents. This may be powerful enough to give her sufficiently positive feelings towards adults and therefore towards God who is (unconsciously if not consciously) conceived of as a super-adult.

The examples of Lee and Lizzie point to a common but important paradox. On one hand, children from loving and accepting non-Christian homes may well come to a robust faith in Christ upon hearing the gospel, for they have experienced from birth what it means to be loved and to trust even though they have not been exposed to Christian teaching. On the other hand, children who have experienced rejection (even in a nominally Christian home) may have immense difficulties in entering into or sustaining a deep faith because, while they may know the content of belief, they have not experienced the kind of human love that opens the way for accepting God's love.

'School' Christianity

A third factor common to our fictional pair, as to most children, is that the bulk of their understanding of the Christian faith has come through school. They do not attend Sunday school and their homes have not seen Christianity as relevant; what they have learned has been passed on by teachers. This has meant that Lee and Lizzie have probably received a very inadequate understanding of faith in Christ, amounting to little more than a collection of Bible stories and woolly inspiration. They are unlikely to have any idea of the core of Christian belief. This is increasingly the case as generations grow up whose parents in turn have little idea of Christianity and are able to pass on to their children only hazy notions at best.

But, more importantly, they have encountered even this watered-down version of Christian faith in a purely *educational* context, which is essentially secular. If, however, one truth stands out from scripture and the life of the church, it is that faith in all its meanings makes sense only in the context of worship. We often forget that the first Christians formulated what they believed and how they should live (faith as believing and doing) as part of worship. They did not sit down and write out systematic works of theology – that came later. They first encountered Christ, worshipped him and then worked out what it meant to live as a Christian.

For Lee and Lizzie, this crucial dimension is missing. They know only *about* Jesus. They do not know his presence in the community of faithful worshippers. The school cannot be expected to fulfil this role. Teachers are not trained or equipped to lead Christian worship and even where (as in Britain) the law requires a daily act of collective worship each day, it merely specifies that 'the majority of acts of worship over a term must be wholly or mainly of a broadly Christian character'[3] and this is sometimes as honoured in the breach as in the observance. Such a situation makes the incorporation of children into the life and worship of the local church absolutely crucial.

Conclusion

The task of evangelists or children's workers, then, is much more complex than simply delivering a gospel talk. They will have to pick up, and make good, the deficiencies of understanding and experience which are the lot of may children today. Ideally, they will be able to recognise what stage of development of faith a child or group of children has reached and shape the message accordingly. For travelling evangelists this will not be easy and they will rely upon detailed information and assessment from local people who know their situation well. This will require careful liaison and planning and above all a local team who are familiar with faith development and who know how to read the situation. Regular children's workers or Sunday school teachers, of course, are in a different position. They will already know their children and, provided there is a willingness and openness to the task of analysis, can set objectives specific to them. Although such work and research may seem complicated and burdensome, it is the only way to develop an effective ministry that is both true to the gospel and true to the ways in which the Holy Spirit may be using the processes of child development to create an appropriate response of faith.

Notes to chapter 4

1   John Inchley, *All About Children*, Eastbourne: Coverdale, 1976, pp 89,90. See also John Inchley, *Realities of Childhood*, London: Scripture Union 1986, pp 122,123.

2   John Westerhoff, *Will Our Children Have Faith?* (revised and expanded edition) Harrisburg, Pa.:Moorehouse Publishing Co., 2000.

3   DFE Circ No 1/94, para 62.

5 The challenging of faith

Adolescence

The years of change

The move to comprehensive school was unlike anything Lee and Lizzie had ever experienced. Whereas they had previously been in a school of 200, they were now among 1,700. Whereas they had been top dogs as Year 6 juniors, they were now lowly Year 7s of whom nobody took much notice. Whereas they had known every teacher in their last school, they now didn't even see half of them. The head teacher was a distant figure, known only as 'Old Mumby' who appeared once a week at lower school assembly. The rest of the time, you saw either your head of year or, in the worst cases, the head of lower school.

In the first two years, Lee's and Lizzie's development carried on much as before. In many ways, they were larger versions of junior age children. But under the surface, major changes were beginning to take place.

Physical change

As they reached the end of the second year it became obvious that, like their companions, they were moving into adolescence. Physically, the transition from child to adult was underway. As soon as this began, Lee's parents introduced him to the facts of life in liaison with the school's programme of sex education. In this way, they were able to make progress together. As usual, however, Lizzie's mum was untroubled. She gave her a booklet and a talking to but beyond that there was no further communication. Fortunately, Wendy's mum had anticipated this and took Lizzie under her wing.

But the physical changes were the least of anybody's difficulties. The 'stormy tunnel of adolescence' had been entered.

Appearance

For Lizzie, this showed itself in an obsession with her appearance. She would spend hours in front of a mirror, checking out that she had the right clothes, make-up and hairstyle. Her mother got tired of it but could do nothing. At first, Lizzie would ask her if she looked all right; it was as if she needed her mother's approval. But since her mother soon made it clear she resented being bothered, Lizzie gradually stopped asking.

Lee's awakening to appearance came later, but when it arrived it was no less fierce. It started with the constant checking and combing of hair. But it quickly progressed to being concerned about all aspects of his appearance. To his parents' surprise, Lee became fashion-conscious and would spend his clothing allowance on the latest jumpers, jeans, jackets and footwear. He did not quite turn into a peacock, but he did become highly sensitive to what people might think of him.

Friendship groups

At the same time, both youngsters (they could hardly be called children any more) attached themselves to specific groups or gangs of 'mates' with whom they went around most of the time. This had begun to happen in earlier years, but it now took a much more distinctive shape.

> What the gang believed, each member believed. What the gang did, each member did. Parents and school had to struggle to gain a hearing at all.

The difference lay in the extent to which each group of friends now claimed the loyalty of its members above all other loyalties. The incident in junior school with Vicki had revealed the beginning of this process. But by the age of thirteen, Lee and Lizzie, in common with everyone else, found their identities no longer mainly in home or school but in relation to their friends.

Previously friends had provided only one among many competing centres of interest and influence; but now they were predominant. What the gang believed, each member believed. What the gang did, each member did. Parents and school had to struggle to gain a hearing at all.

The most amusing example of this had been over the question of earrings. The school allowed neither boys nor girls to wear them. But one day, Shaun, a member of Lee's circle, arrived sporting a ring in his left ear. He was told to remove it, whereupon he found it promptly confiscated. The next day Shaun reappeared with another ring. However, it had become not only Shaun this time, but half the class. By the end of the week, Mr Simmons the class teacher had over fifty rings in his drawer. As he put it to his colleagues in the staff room, 'The herd instinct has taken over again from school rules or common sense.'

The same applied to questions of belief. When one person in the class announced she was turning to astrology, so did everyone else. For two weeks, the only topic of conversation was horoscopes and astral signs. If you did not know your birth sign or did not believe the horoscope you were definitely out in the cold.

This intensity of belonging to a group meant that in just about every matter of significance, it was the group's view that counted. The views of teachers or parents were all subsidiary. In any clash, it was always the group that won the loyalty of its members.

Rows and questions

At home this led to enormous rows. Lizzie, who by this time had come to reject her mother intensely, clashed with her on several occasions. It was on one of these that her mother shouted that she wished Lizzie had never been born. Lizzie screamed back that she had not asked to be brought into the world and at this her mother withdrew her harsh words. But, inwardly, Lizzie knew that they had only given voice to what they had both felt for years. The rejection she had felt from birth had been brought out into the open. It was never to be healed.

Lee, meanwhile, had begun to question just about everything his parents believed in or stood for. He no longer wanted to do things as part of the family. He did not want to identify with the community association of which they were members (he had always enjoyed their social events in the past). And he did not want to go on holiday with them. He wanted more freedom of choice in what he wore, how he looked and when he was to come in at night. In short, he became the typical rebellious teenager.

At school, both Lee and Lizzie fitted into the system but were careful to distance themselves from it. Like most of their friends, they were decidedly 'standoff-ish' towards it.

There was, however, one exception to this for each of them. Lizzie did not care for most teachers (they were part of 'the system') but she did like Mrs Hampton, her English teacher. This was largely because she allowed Lizzie the freedom to escape. Lizzie had always liked stories and, even at junior school, had used them as a means of escape. Now, with things becoming worse at home, Lizzie found relief in literature. Mrs Hampton realised this and sympathised. Moreover, when it came to setting study projects for homework, she would agree to Lizzie's request not to study books with a plot majoring on family life; it was simply too painful. At the same time, Lizzie agreed to see the school counsellor as part of the deal.

As a result, Lizzie liked and respected Mrs Hampton. Her homework was always in on time and well presented. Its quality was high too. The approval she sought from home and which was not forthcoming (her mum never came to open evenings at the school), Lizzie now found in a combination of Mrs Hampton and Wendy's mum and dad, who more than ever had become surrogate parents.

Lee likewise found an alternative parent in the person of Mr Payne the sports teacher. At first sight, this seemed a bit strange since Lee hated sport. He was no good at it and would do anything to get out of games periods, including falsifying sickness notes and feigning illness. Mr Payne, however, saw through all this but would have none of it. One afternoon, while the class were out on a cross country run, he took Lee to one side and found out what the problem was. It had happened that as a young child, Lee had needed an operation on his leg. This left him with a poor sense of balance and co-ordination. It had also left an unsightly scar. On both counts Lee was deeply embarrassed in front of the class. He always had been, but it was worse now.

Mr Payne's remedy was to arrange for Lee to see a sports physiotherapist and then to give Lee some special training sessions after school and a schedule of exercises for use at home. Within a matter of weeks, the combination of physiotherapy, personal attention and proper training had developed skills Lee never dreamt he had. He would not become the star of the school football team; but he learned to play a decent game and was selected to play for the school reserves.

One result was that although the rebellious streak remained, Lee became much more settled. At home he rejoined family activities and even volunteered to run a stall at the community association's summer fête. His parents heaved a sigh of relief and hoped that the peak of teenage turbulence had passed.

The struggle for identity

This brief sketch of the early years of adolescence carries us to the limit of our study. By their mid-teens, Lee, Lizzie and the thousands like them can hardly be called children. And yet in vital ways they are. The teenage years bring discontinuity with what has gone before, but they also reveal a considerable amount of continuity. Teenagers do not suddenly cease to be all that they have been previously. Adolescence builds on the experiences of childhood; it does not erase them.

> Teenagers do not suddenly cease to be all that they have been previously. Adolescence builds on the experiences of childhood: it does not erase them.

But, as any parent will know, adolescence introduces developments and problems which are of a different order from those of childhood. The biggest of these is the *struggle for identity*. James Fowler has described puberty as a time of mirrors.[1] Teenagers are constantly preoccupied with image. This takes its most obvious form in an incessant concern for how they *look*: 'Is my hair all right? Does this jacket fit? Is it fashionable? Do my spots show?' The sensitivity of a teenager to what will later seem trivial is unbounded.

Self discovery

The outward, however, is only half the story. It is the inward struggle for identity which acts as the driving force behind the anxieties that beset these years. This, in itself, is part of the process of mirroring. For at the same time as adolescents ask whether their outward appearance is acceptable, they are also asking what others think of them as persons. They are not only trying to find out how they look; they want to know whether others like them too. As Fowler puts it: '[the teenager] needs the eyes and ears of a few trusted others in which to see the image of personality emerging.'

This attempt by the teenager to construct or find an identity combines with the hormonal and other physical changes which accompany puberty. Together these forces create the inner turbulence and even violence experienced from twelve or thirteen years onwards. For the first time in their lives, teenagers are confronted with the question, 'Who am I?' Both their physical and mental growth tell them that they are growing up fast. But for what? And into what? It is a frightening time as each day brings new changes in body and mood, both of which seem uncontrollable. In all of this the experiences of the past will be influencing the processes of the present, as he or she struggles to create a new identity out of the old.

Models of adolescence

There are two ways of looking at this teenage identity crisis, though the one does not exclude aspects of the other:

- The first sees adolescence as an *explosion*. This is apt in many ways because the characteristics of an explosion – its force, its potential for destruction, its raw power – are precisely those which are present in puberty.

  Yet even here we must draw a distinction. There are controlled as well as uncontrolled explosions. The identity crisis of the teenage years is not always unpredictable or destructive. For instance, it is predictable in that we know everyone experiences it in generally similar ways. And it can usually be contained, provided that wise parents and others know what is going on and so build in safety valves. It may be explosive but it does not have to destroy everything in its path.

- The second way of looking at puberty is to compare it to a *chrysalis*. This may seem too gentle given that we have already likened it to an explosion. But the comparison is nevertheless valid. It conveys the ideas of transition, growth and emergence – the features of the chrysalis as it moves from being a caterpillar to becoming a butterfly – and the characteristics of teenhood. The boy or girl who enters puberty in Year 8 or 9 of comprehensive school is not the same boy or girl who emerges from it in Year 11 or 12.

This process of self-discovery is always painful. But it is doubly so if we have never been sure of those who gave us selfhood in the first place. This is why Lizzie found it so difficult. Prior to adolescence, her identity had been formed for her by a combination of relationships given to her *'from the outside'* – her family, her class at school, her gang of friends and so on. But now she is discovering an identity that springs from within as she begins to ask herself questions about meaning and purpose.

In this situation, our feelings may assure us that there is meaning and purpose to our existence because we sense that we have been valued in our own right from the beginning of our lives. We would not have been born otherwise. We are here because someone wanted us to be here and therefore our lives began with a loving purpose. For Lizzie and children like her, however, her deepest feelings tell her nothing of the kind. If they tell her anything it is that she has never been wanted by those who brought her into the world. For her there are no memories of soft words and cuddles to reassure her that there is meaning and purpose, and that she is loved.

It is at this point that the covenantal love of babyhood once again becomes crucial. Lizzie is not as desperate as some because she has found an alternative source of warmth and care in Wendy's family. But even these will not completely erase the pain of rejection by those who were responsible for her entry into the world (a decision over which she had no control and for which she has suffered ever since).

Ability to reflect

A second factor in the search for identity is the more developed ability of the teenager to reflect. We noted earlier that junior children are able to order their thoughts and experience in narrative form but that they usually operate from within the stream of the story. ('I did this, then we did that'- and so on). With adolescence comes a greater ability to stand back from the flow and reflect upon it. We can compare these two stages to a stream. Junior children are in the stream. Even when they are recounting what goes on, they are generally doing so while standing in the middle of it rather than looking at it from any other standpoint. Teenagers, however, are more able to stand on the bank and comment on what is happening even when they remain part of the flow. It is as if they have developed the capacity to observe themselves through the eyes of a spectator.

This is what 'the time of mirrors' means. Teenagers standing on the bank are worried about what others may think of them as they, too, stand on the bank. They are continually anxious about image.

The 'others' who matter, however, are no longer those who mattered during childhood. Parents must take a back seat. Those whose opinions are sought are increasingly teenage peers. It is contemporaries whom they want to impress, not their elders.

The incident with the earrings was a classic example of this, as were the 'herd' reactions to astrology and sporting ability. Lee's loathing of sport was not just a question of embarrassment about his scar (after all, he had played games at junior school) but resulted from a keen awareness that the majority were good at sport while he wasn't. It was better not to take part than to look a fool, even if this meant deception.

> ## Parents must take a back seat. Those whose opinions are sought are increasingly teenage peers.

Intellectual growth

Emotions and physique, however, are not all there is to puberty. In earlier stages of development we notice intellectual changes too. Is there a corresponding shift in teenage years?

The answer is yes, but not in the same way. The key development in early teenage understanding is the ability to move from concrete to abstract thinking. For example, at junior school Lizzie translated the abstract concept of justice into concrete terms of helping children injured by landmines. Now she would be able to reverse the procedure. Faced with a specific situation, she would be able to say whether or not it was just, according to how well it conformed to an abstract notion of justice.

This shift in mental ability is frequently uneven and patchy. Not all adolescents reach the same level of abstraction. Some move only a little way beyond the concrete stage. And it is a fact that vast numbers of adults remain stuck in early adolescence for most of their lives. Hence the popularity of tabloid newspapers written entirely around concrete ways of thinking.

Emotionally and intellectually, therefore, teenagers undergo nothing short of a revolution. What implications does this have for evangelism?

Evangelistic implications

Affiliative faith

In contrast to the period of 'experienced faith' which marked the infant and junior years, the adolescent moves into what Westerhoff has called *affiliative faith*.[2] This is marked by three features:

- *Identifying with the faith of friends*
  Firstly, the teenager joins himself to, and identifies with, the 'faith' of his friends. This may not be Christian faith at all. It may be trivial astrology, agnosticism, pleasure-seeking or whatever. Or, if his friends are mainly Christians, it may be Christianity. The fact is that he will identify with what his friends accept rather than find an individually thought-out faith for himself. It is the herd instinct at work.

- *Dominance of feelings*
  The second feature of affiliative faith is found in the dominance of feelings and affections. In the swirl of emotions and changing perceptions, feelings come to control everything. It is what *feels* OK that counts, irrespective of intellectual coherence or integrity.

- *Questioning authority*
  Thirdly, there is the question of authority. This no longer resides in adults or institutions, pure and simple. Authority, religious or otherwise, must gain the right to be heard and obeyed by submitting itself to inspection. If it does not conform to the teenager's sense of values or priorities, it will not be accepted as worthwhile. An authority – that of the school, for instance – may enforce *acceptance* by virtue of its power; but it will not win the *allegiance* of the adolescent who does

not agree that its rule is valid. The most it can do is hope to enforce conformity.

The stage of affiliative faith, then, is one in which the evangelist will have to fight even to get a hearing. We all know the youth club syndrome where teenagers happily give themselves to recreational activities but switch off during the epilogue. The 'God slot' becomes the price to pay for having somewhere to meet as a group.

The evangelist's reaction

How should we react to this? In the end it boils down to two alternatives: we can either try to undermine the affiliative instinct or we can work with it. Many of the problems encountered by workers with this age group arise because of a failure or refusal to acknowledge the importance of the affiliative stage. We try to usher adolescents into individual (essentially adult) ways of thinking and behaviour for which they are not yet ready. That will come in the next stage.

The answer almost certainly is to 'go with the flow': to accept that thirteen to sixteen year olds are going to find their identities in gangs or groups, and construct a programme which reflects this. This will mean becoming a member of the group with all its obligations and loyalties. It is no good trying to be a wolf in sheep's clothing, pretending to be in tune with the affiliations of the group when all along you only want to fit its members into an adult mould.

In practical terms, this will mean working and playing with the group in a relationship of equals. Although the evangelist may *suggest* a structure of activities, say, during a holiday club week, if she is wise she will not *impose* it. She will be ready to accept the overruling of the group provided a constructive alternative is proposed, and she will be very wary of invoking the notion of authority.

In terms of what to teach, much will depend upon the intellectual stage of the group. In the early teens, there is a fine balance to be struck between the concrete and the abstract. In any case, abstract concepts need to be well illustrated even for adults, so it will be better to err on the side of concreteness than abstraction. What is clear, however, is that simply talking *at* teenagers is more often than not counter-productive. Although they may be willing to accept the gospel from someone they like and respect, they will not swallow teaching simply because the evangelist 'says so'.

Evaluating responses

The result of all this will be variable. In some cases, there will be no response. In others, we may discover a strong response. But just as we need to exercise wisdom and discernment in evaluating responses made by juniors, so we need to do the same towards teenagers. For an adolescent who seems to make a commitment to Christ may be doing one or a combination of things:

- responding to an adult he has come to like and respect and whom he wants to please;
- following the herd or the example of a friend;
- seeking an answer to his identity crises;
- trying to discover a new affiliative group to which he can belong;
- seeking Christ as the Spirit leads him into repentance and faith.

None of these can be excluded and most commitments probably include an element of each. The important point is that if we have an understanding of the features of affiliative faith, we shall be better equipped to interpret a teenager's response. If we do not, there is a good chance we shall naively misread the situation and mishandle it.

> We have to be prepared to watch teenagers apparently move in and out of faith as their identities and affiliations switch back and forth.

More problematically, this means that we have to be prepared to watch teenagers apparently move in and out of faith as their identities and affiliations switch back and forth. When faced with this situation, it is tempting to apply adult categories and chide them for backsliding, or question their sincerity. Although there may be times when this is necessary, the nature of adolescent development means this need not be a permanent state of affairs but can lead on to something more stable and long-lasting. Godly patience and a love of butterflies are perhaps the qualities most to be sought by the Christian worker with teenagers.

When does faith development end?

We have reached the end of Lee's and Lizzie's life stories. Or at least, that part which is relevant to this book. They are now sixteen or seventeen and to all intents and purposes have become young adults. In a year or two's time the law will recognise them fully as adults and accord them the right to vote, marry, and fight for their country.

But it is not the end of their development as persons or in faith. How they might develop in either realm would require a book of its own. On any model of growth, they still have a long way to go.

To leave their stories at this point, however, would be to exit at the most crucial time. It would be like getting to the ultimate cliffhanger in a novel – only to discover that the publisher had decided to print no more pages!

What follows in this chapter is not the definitive 'plot' for the rest of Lee's and Lizzie's lives, but a sketching of possibilities. Although patterns have emerged in the course of their childhood and adolescence, the exact direction in which these will go cannot be predicted in advance. When we have got as far as models of human and faith development can take us, a number of stages still lie ahead. Moreover, there are many variable choices and possibilities within these stages. Lee and Lizzie may choose one or a combination of them; their choices are not determined in advance.

> They may simply travel through life
> stuck at the stage of development they
> reached by late teens.

One distinct possibility has to be borne in mind: *they may not go through any further stages of development at all*. They may simply travel through life stuck at the stage of development they reached by late teens. This is a common phenomenon; large numbers of adults do not get very far past the concrete thinking stage in intellectual development. This is why political organisations cast their messages in concrete terms. People do not want to discuss the abstract rights and wrongs of large-scale issues; they want to know how they will be affected in their daily lives.

In the same way, it is probably true to say that in religion the majority of the population does not move beyond the affiliative faith stage of early adolescence. Whether we define faith as believing, trusting or doing, the fact is that few people have a faith that amounts to more than the consensus of view held by their companions. It is not quite as crude as the herd instinct but it is not far off.

So we find that in a mass democracy such as Britain, Australia or the United States, where the influence of the media is all-pervasive, there are *general* views about Christianity as about everything else. Those who have a carefully worked-out faith for themselves, who will stand up when others around them are saying something different, are few and far between.

Lee and Lizzie may go through further stages of growth, then, or they may not. In the remainder of this chapter, we shall look at what these might be. For the definitive conclusion to the Lee and Lizzie saga, however, the reader will have to fall back upon his or her own literary talents.

Further faith developments

John Westerhoff has suggested that if there is to be full development of faith a person will go through four stages.[1] Stage one is that of *experienced faith*, which, as we have seen, is crucial in babyhood and infancy. Stage two is the time of *affiliative faith*, when children (and some adults who never move beyond this stage) believe what their friends or family believe but have not yet come to a thought-out faith for themselves. Stage three he describes as *searching faith*, and stage four as *owned faith*. We have already observed the characteristics of experienced and affiliative faith. It remains for us to see what is meant by searching and owned faith.

Searching faith

This comes typically in late teens (although it may come as late as the thirties or not at all). Since searching faith and conversion frequently go hand in hand, however, and since the majority of conversions take place in teenage years, we shall locate it earlier rather than later.

As teenagers develop a sense of identity, new questions and doubts crop up. They become dissatisfied with previous answers to questions of meaning and purpose. Moreover, they find that going along with the faith of the crowd is inadequate; they must have their own answers, not somebody else's. They are therefore increasingly driven on by questions across the whole range of life.

James Fowler has pointed out that the person moving into the searching stage is often someone who belongs to a community or group which has a strong sense of identity and beliefs. These may become too rigid or out of touch with the rest of the searcher's experience for him to accept them any longer. A good example of this would be a teenager who grows up in a rigid evangelical home and church but has never experienced anything wider or different. He has made a public profession of faith because that seemed natural. But in fact, his faith is still at the affiliative stage. At some point he encounters other people, beliefs or situations which challenge his upbringing (at university for instance). But because he has only ever moved in circles which have reinforced his beliefs and not questioned them, he does not have the equipment to meet the new challenge. His profession of faith was sincere but it did not develop out of struggle and is not adequate to cope with the questions which now assail him.

This leads to experimentation. Because his previous set of beliefs and values are now unable to supply what he wants, he may dip into a wide variety of philosophies and cultures. The search for truth may lead him into all kinds of practices which he will later come to disown or regret, such as mysticism, cults, astrology, drugs. At least, the searcher will explore beyond the bounds of his earlier assumptions as he examines the claims of other religions, politics and lifestyles.

But this searching is not just intellectual. There is an emotional searching as well: a need for commitment to persons and causes: Oxfam, socialism, the poor, liberty, democracy, to mention but a few. The searcher is looking for someone or something to give himself to, which in return will give him meaning and purpose.

We can see how different searching faith is from what has gone before. The searcher is much more conscious of himself as an individual made for meaning and purpose. He is no longer content to live on the surface of life, eating, drinking and making merry. He has moved beyond the point where superficial pleasure for its own sake contains any answers. He must find something which touches the depths of his being.

So far, the searcher has been self-centered. Not in an immoral way, but he has been concerned to find truth that will make sense for *him*. Westerhoff now introduces a factor which will turn the searcher away from himself. He calls this 'the act of surrender'.

When the searcher surrenders himself to a belief or cause, he acknowledges with his heart and mind that meaning lies outside himself and lays a claim upon him. He is jolted into accepting that he is not the beginning and end of everything and that in order to find true meaning and purpose he must stop acting as if he were. This is the essence of surrender and leads directly to the fourth stage, *owned faith*.

Owned faith

The act of surrender opens the door to a new way of believing. The light has dawned, the penny has dropped. The world will never be the same again. The searcher has found faith for *himself*, not as one of a crowd, not as the recipient of something handed down but as an individual making a personal discovery that changes his life. But we need to note that owned faith does not only apply to Christianity. The process of searching and the act of surrender can lead to other kinds of commitment, both religious and non-religious. What characterises all of them is their shared *forms* of experience, irrespective of their *content*.

To recognise this is not the same as saying that all faiths are equal. From a biblical point of view, the content and object of faith make all the difference. To believe in astrology is not to believe in Christ by another name.

But from the standpoint of *how* we come to believe (in anything), we see the processes of faith development in members of political parties who have given themselves wholly to the cause in which they believe; in sportsmen who have made their commitment to sport the centre of their lives; in those who have devoted their energies to community life and action. We see it, too, in members of other religions who, like the committed Christian, have moved beyond superficial adherence into heartfelt faith.

The owned faith of these individuals is every bit as real as full-hearted Christianity, though Christians would dispute the claim that the object of their faith was as worthy. The task of the evangelist is not to disparage such commitment but to preach Christ in such a way that his hearers may come to own a new faith in him.

One other point needs perhaps to be reiterated. In discussing models of faith development, it is important to remember that although the human processes and stages may be similar whatever the content of faith, the Christian model understands faith in Christ to be the outcome of the divine work of the Holy Spirit. It is not simply a matter of human processes. God's Spirit is supernaturally at work, bringing about conviction and understanding of spiritual truths. As St Paul makes clear, we come to saving faith in Jesus (whatever age we may be) because God takes the scales from our eyes, not because we remove them ourselves. This needs always to be kept in the forefront of our minds as we learn from the insights of faith development theorists.

> When the searcher surrenders himself to a belief or cause, he acknowledges with his heart and mind that meaning lies outside himself and lays a claim upon him.

Conclusion

We have looked in some detail at how children can be said to have faith, and have seen that it is possible to speak of faith in diverse, though connected, ways. Equally important, we have noted that a child's response of faith is not the same as that of an adult. Rather, he or she moves through stages of development, each of which (as we have seen) has its own characteristic response.

In all this, it needs to be stressed that whether we are talking about faith developmentally or theologically, we are still talking about faith as a gift from God. It is so because all God's creation must be regarded as a gift. It is not something which just happens to 'be there'; it is the deliberate handiwork of a loving Father.

When, therefore, we speak of children 'naturally' possessing faith, we are not speaking of something which has happened independently of God. He is the sustainer as well as creator of the natural processes, and a child's capacity to respond to the world around her and to persons (even God himself) is as much a gift as the lakes, mountains and valleys. A child's response to nature may, without her realising it, be a response to the God who created nature and who has made us in his own image. We must never drive a wedge between creation and salvation: it is the same God who has brought about both. Both are aspects of his loving purpose and it is God's Spirit who prompts the response of faith to both.

We can begin to see, then, that there are some questions which can only be answered theologically: What do we mean by speaking of creation and salvation as being tied together? How does Jesus Christ and his work of atonement fit into this? What do we mean by 'sin' if children's behaviour is determined by the natural process of development? Does this rule out accountability before God? And what about conversion? Is there any room for it within stages of faith?

These are just some of the big issues we shall be considering in part two of this book. Others will include: the use of adult power; children and worship (especially in the context of Holy Communion), the relationship between believing and belonging; and children and spiritual gifts. In the chapters that follow, we shall be concerned with the biblical and theological perspectives and principles that should undergird good practice rather than the 'nuts and bolts' of organising such practice.

It will not be possible to arrive at final answers, for theology is not like a Sherlock Holmes puzzle. We must remain open to the possibility that God will modify and even overturn our fallible human views. The best we can do is to submit both our questions and provisional answers to him and his word in the knowledge that he is faithful and will lead us into all truth.

Notes to chapter 5

1   James Fowler, *Stages of Faith*, New York, Harper & Row 1981, p151.
2   John Westerhoff, *Will Our Children Have Faith?* (revised and expanded edition) Harrisburg Pa.: Moorehouse Publishing Co., 2000
3   Westerhoff, as above.

Part Two

A Continuing Agenda

6 Faith development, sin and accountability

A s we saw with Lee and Lizzie, a child's awareness of the world around her develops over time. The same is true of her awareness of God. Theologically, we may say that she is created in God's image and with an instinct for him – as Augustine put it, with a God-shaped gap which only God can fill.

How this develops will be affected by crucial factors outside the child's control. Her family, for example, may be opposed to Christian faith or, alternatively, simply not interested. Since the family is the most important context for nurture and growth, its attitude will be determinative for the child's faith development. Other important factors will be the attitude of teachers, friends and the media.

But in all this we have to recognise that children are not simply conditioned automatons devoid of their own wills. Though they will be conditioned to some extent, we must acknowledge both pragmatically and theologically that they retain some ability to choose, whether in the area of relationships, values or simple obedience and disobedience to rules. It is in this context that the problem of sin and accountability which has preoccupied children's evangelists for so long must be discussed.

What is sin?

A sk the legendary man or woman in the street what they understand by sin and you almost certainly get a list of actions to avoid: the seven (or more) deadly sins. But this is misleading. In scripture, particularly in the writings of Paul, we find sin portrayed not so much as a series of specific offences as in terms of: (1) a power which controls us; and (2) a state in which we find ourselves.

Sin as a power

Both Jesus and Paul viewed sin as an occupying power that conquers and enslaves us. In John 8:34, Jesus declares, 'I tell you the truth, everyone who sins is a slave to sin.' Likewise, Paul declares that 'all men are ... under the power of sin' (Romans 3:9 RSV) and speaks of Christians as once having been 'slaves to sin' (Romans 6:6). Addressed to believers in Rome, the image was doubly powerful for they knew exactly what slavery entailed.

Sin, thus pictured, can be compared to the slavemaster who cracks the whip over us at will. We are in bondage to him and cannot escape. Our lives are controlled by his harsh and cruel demands.

Our individual acts of sin are the evidence of his control. It is not that we are declared sinful because we commit sins. We sin because we are already controlled by the power of sin. The particular sins we engage in are simply the fruit of the principle of sin that is at work within us.

We live as if God did not matter.

This is a crucial point of Christian doctrine. There are many people (some of them Christians) who believe that to be right with God is essentially a matter of ceasing to commit acts of sin. They are like the smoker who thinks that his problem will be solved by not buying cigarettes. But this is to miss the point. Sin, like smoking, is a question of addiction. It is not the individual items that have to be given up: it is the power or grip behind them which has to be dealt with.

An illustration from nature may help. Ask yourself what makes a cat a hunter. Is it the individual prey she catches, or does she catch the prey because she is by instinct already a hunter? The answer, of course, is that she hunts because it is part of her being. Bringing home a mouse or a bird does not make her a hunter: she hunts them because she is a hunter by nature. She would not be a cat otherwise.

This parallels our experience of sin. We sin because we are by nature sinners. We are not made sinners because we commit acts of sin. It is the

occupying, controlling power of sin that makes us sinful and which must
be destroyed.

Sin as a state

We are not only sinners by nature, we are sinners by choice. Sin therefore describes both the power that enslaves us and the state we find
ourselves in before God. In Romans, Paul paints a picture of humanity
having deliberately turned away from God. This chimes with Luther's
description of us as being 'curved in upon ourselves'. We are oriented
towards self and selfishness. This is what lies at the heart of idolatry:

> '... what may be known about God is plain to them
> [humanity], because God has made it plain to them. For
> since the creation of the world God's invisible qualities –
> his eternal power and divine nature – have been clearly
> seen, being understood from what has been made, so that
> men are without any excuse.
>
> For although they knew God, they neither glorified him as
> God nor gave thanks to him, but their thinking became
> futile and their foolish hearts were darkened ... They
> exchanged the truth of God for a lie and worshipped and
> served created things rather than the Creator...' (Romans
> 1:19–21, 25).

The logic of Paul's argument runs like this: through creation, we have
known enough about God to acknowledge our dependence upon him and
to realise that he has a claim upon us. But we (the human race) want to
be independent of God. So we seek wisdom and security in creation and
in human affairs. We live as if God did not matter. This has several disastrous results.

*Firstly, we end up worshipping anything and everything other than
God.* By worship, Paul does not mean that we literally bow down before
our cars, our possessions, our families and so on. He means that we give
something other than God the central place in our lives. Whatever form
it takes, it becomes an idol.

Secondly, the rejection of God leads to immorality. Again, Paul is not
suggesting that everyone becomes a murderer or a thief. He is trying to
show that society without God will find itself afflicted by all kinds of

immorality because inborn sinfulness will rise up and take control.

Thirdly, once sin gains an entry it multiplies. Individually and socially, the human race becomes trapped in a downward spiral of ever-increasing speed. Even if it wanted to free itself (which it doesn't), it could not.

It is at this point that voluntary sin is transformed into sin the slave-master. What began as a deliberate choice now becomes an inescapable trap. The power of sin reigns.

All this means that our state of supposed independence is, in fact, the worst kind of bondage. For we are not only spiralling away from God and all that is good, but we do so in the illusion that it represents true freedom! It is little wonder that in 2 Corinthians 4:4, Paul describes this as blindness.

> We are not only spiralling away from God and all that is good, but we do so in the illusion that it represents true freedom!

A broken relationship

We need to note one further point. At bottom, sin is not a matter of breaking impersonal laws set up by an impersonal divine legislature. It is the breaking of a personal relationship with God. When we sin he is pained by the breach of friendship this entails. The Old Testament prophets saw this clearly. They characterise sin as the breaking of the covenant between Yahweh and his people. Israel's sin is tantamount to adultery – the breaking of the most intimate bond of all (Hosea 2,3). The cry of the heartbroken husband echoes in God's word to Hosea: ' "She [Israel] decked herself with rings and jewellery, and went after her lovers, but me she forgot," declares the Lord.' (Hosea 2:13). This – the deliberate breach of relationship – is what lies at the heart of sin.

Theology versus social science?

Whether we think of sin as a power or as a state, it is clear that the plight of humanity is desperate. We are gripped by the force of sin and held in a state which cuts us off from God and renders us worthy of condemnation. It amounts to a broken relationship that is not just the result of a falling out between human beings and God, but a full-scale rebellion. The end result will be either reconciliation or rejection.

How should we match this with the findings of child development? And what are the implications for evangelism?

We are faced with two sets of facts. One is *theological*: it tells us about the human condition viewed from a biblical perspective. Its primary concern is to set out the relationship of humanity to God, though in doing so, it also speaks of the disrupted nature of relationships within the human race. The other is drawn from the *social sciences*. Its concern is to explain what we know (or think we know) about the observable processes of human development. It is not necessarily anti-theological but it has been used in this way. For this reason, many Christians are profoundly and understandably suspicious.

This has been unfortunate. It has led to evangelism and Christian nurture being uninformed by the study of how children develop. And in reverse, it has led to the assumption on the part of some developmentalists that the Christian faith has nothing to say of any value.

These two forms of exclusivism have impoverished ministry to children. It is conceivable that they have done real damage to children's spiritual growth. In refusing to take account of each other, they have either ignored vital spiritual truths or they have disparaged the new knowledge we have steadily gained about how children grow up. There is much to be repented of on both sides: the evangelist who says that he has nothing to learn from the developmentalist is no less guilty than the developmentalist who declares the Christian faith to be irrelevant. Openness and humility are needed on both sides.

A compartmentalist model tries to take account of this but it offers few practical ways forward. Its strength is that it recognises the importance of both theology and child development. But its weakness is that it fails to show how they are related. So, for example, theology governs the religious life while psychology governs the mental one. It can only say that each is a truthful account in its own way and invite us to choose whichever we want.

The integrationist view, however, is not satisfied with such an approach. It seeks to find a means of applying both theological and developmental insights without putting them into separate boxes. How does this work out in practice?

Humans as sinners: an integrationist approach

Let us take the idea of humans as sinners. If we compare the teaching of Paul with the arguments of modern psychologists, we seem to have two contradictory and incompatible positions. Whereas Paul speaks of human beings choosing sin, a psychologist may well speak of the irresistable and uncontrollable forces within us which determine our behaviour. Whereas Paul may describe human beings as having deliberately rejected God in favour of self-reliance, the psychologist may claim that the notions of independence and self-confidence are essential to healthy personality. Whereas Paul condemns self-centredness, the psychologist may reply that from birth we are necessarily conditioned to look after number one and that if we did not do so we would not survive. And so on.

> Whereas Paul condemns self-centredness, the psychologist may reply that from birth we are necessarily conditioned to look after number one and that if we did not do so we would not survive.

The integrationist approach can therefore seem doomed from the start. It would appear that we are not just describing the same thing differently, but that we are faced with two incompatible accounts of what sin actually is.

But is this necessarily true? The first point to note is that although Paul describes the effects of sin, he nowhere gives a detailed explanation of the processes involved beyond the combination of theology and common sense contained in Romans 6 and 7. Even there he is concerned primarily with the spiritual and theological dimensions.

What is equally striking, however, is that neither in his review of how the human race came to choose sin (Romans 1) nor in his discussion of how sin entered through Adam (Romans 5), does Paul attempt to explain exactly the means by which these happened. He is content to state in a broad way that we have deliberately chosen sin rather than God and that Adam's sin represents the human race's first such choice; but Paul does not venture beyond that. His primary goal is to enable his readers to make *theological* sense of their *personal experience* of sin and to understand that in Christ there is freedom and reconciliation. Although he shows deep psychological insight, Paul is not interested in being an early developmental psychologist.

If we accept this, we are freed to look again at the developmental evidence. We can begin by asking what the explanations of child development and behaviour are trying to do. The answer is that they are trying to give an account of how we grow up and the kind of common patterns that are observable in children's experience. *In themselves,* these accounts do not rule out God's involvement: if such an assumption is made, it is the result of a *prior* decision to exclude theology, or to relegate the activity of God to a supernatural plane, strictly separated from the natural.

In giving an account or accounts of human growth, the social scientist is simply putting observable characteristics into some kind of pattern and trying to suggest how they have come to be.

An example

Imagine that a child has stolen some sweets. He is from a poor home with unloving parents and his older brother has recently been convicted of theft. What do we make of his actions?

1 *Did he know stealing was wrong?* If he did not, then he can hardly be put in the same category as a child who knows what theft is and still goes ahead with it. If he did, however, we must suppose that, assuming he was not forced to steal by a parent, brother or bully, he could have chosen not to and therefore must be held accountable for his actions.
2 *What led him to steal?* Was it greed, poverty, trying to impress his friends, or what? Here the psychologist can be of great help. He may point to the child's poor home, or the fact that everyone in his home steals and so the child has simply acquired what he wants in the way all his family do. Nevertheless, if he knew theft was wrong and chose it still, he is accountable.

We can hold theft to be a sin, therefore, but still recognise the role of psychological factors in leading a person to sin. The non-theological account of how the sin arose does not invalidate the theological significance of the action: theft is sin, but extenuating circumstances may modify our attitude to questions of responsibility and punishment so that, for example, the child may be warned rather than prosecuted.

Original sin: matching theology and development

Another way of looking at integration is to try to match the theological and developmental accounts feature by feature. This may not be possible at all points but there are some where it is. To demonstrate, we shall focus on the idea of original sin.

Although Paul nowhere uses the term 'original sin', the notion of inborn sinfulness is prominent in his thinking. Indeed, that is the idea behind Paul's discussion of Adam and Christ in Romans 5: we all share in Adam's sinfulness and are therefore slaves to sin. When we look at what inborn sinfulness is we find that the ideas of theology and psychology come very close to each other, although they do not use the same language.

At the core of Paul's definition of sin lies the notion of self-centredness: Luther's idea of being curved in upon oneself. It is not just that we care about ourselves but that we are concerned for ourselves *above all else*. When the chips are down, it is number one that counts. Even when the chips are not down, we seek to gain the most for ourselves out of any situation, even at the expense of others.

But, of course, self-centredness also has a God-ward aspect. We desire to elevate ourselves into God's place and to live independently of him, fashioning him after our own image. This is being curved in on oneself with a vengeance.

The developmentalist will say that such self-centred behaviour is characteristic of all young children. As we noticed in the cases of Lee and Lizzie, the first months and years of life are built upon the perception that the world revolves around supplying the infant's needs. In this sense there is an inborn self-centredness in us all. It is part of what it means to be human.

But that is exactly Paul's point: to be human is to be born sinful because to be born human means to be born self-centred in relation to God and to others. Paul and modern psychology both agree that self-centredness is a trait we are all born with. So the developmentalist's observable evidence of inborn self-centredness corresponds to Paul's theological idea of inborn sinfulness.

Paul and modern psychology both agree that self-centredness is a trait we are all born with.

At what point does inborn sinfulness or self-centredness become deliberate sin? Here again, we find a match between theology and psychology. In addition to viewing sin as a power and a state, Paul characterises sinfulness in two further ways. On one hand it is a *rejection of God* and, on the other, a *lack of love for other people*. The psychologists may have nothing to say about the first, but it is the view of all psychological theories that healthy personal development is achieved only by learning to respect others. Put another way, the mature individual is one who relates to other people not because of what they can *supply* but because of what they *are* - valuable persons in their own right. And the healthiest community is one in which people do things for one another out of generosity.

The self-centredness of natural growth first becomes wilful sin, then, when we deliberately choose to elevate our own desires above those of others. This involves, of course, the capacity to recognise the existence of other people's rights. As we shall see in our discussion of accountability, such a capacity does not develop *fully* until teenage years. But once it becomes possible to say, 'That person has equal rights to mine but I shall do my utmost to make sure that I always come off best', the threshold of wilful sin has been crossed. We have all met children as well as adults who are simply 'users' of others. Even when they appear to care for somebody else, it is still essentially a route to personal advancement. Such people are exaggerated forms of what we all are: sinners curved in upon ourselves.

The relationship of theology and child development, therefore, can be shown to be complementary provided the limitations and claims of each are understood. There will be occasions when it becomes difficult to see how they match. But the proper response at that point should not be to reject one in favour of the other or to say that one is superior to the other. It should be either to accept that their relationship is not clear and live with the gap between them, or to keep on working at a resolution. Given that both have valuable insights into the human condition, it would be irresponsible to write off one simply because at first glance there seem to be elements that cannot be reconciled.

Sin and accountability

The question of what we should make of sin leads us into another crucial area. Whenever children's workers get together to discuss theology, one question above all comes to dominate the discussion: the spiritual status of the child. This is hardly surprising since a children's worker will find that the position he or she takes on this issue will determine the goal of his or her ministry. In this section we shall look at the main views in the debate, from the standpoint of accountability and responsibility and ask how far these concepts are applicable to children and therefore what follows in terms of communicating the gospel.

An age of accountability

The problem of child accountability has been recognised for a long time. The traditional answer has been given in terms of an *age of accountability*. Ron Buckland in his book *Children and the King*, defines this as 'usually understood in negative terms, ie as a time when the child, if he rejects Christ, is open to the just judgment of God.'[1]

The notion of a fixed and specific point of accountability, however, has come under fire. One children's evangelist summed up the feelings of many when he commented that, 'Any attempt to pinpoint a moment in the life of a child as being the actual age of accountability will be met with disappointment'[2] and was happier to speak of a 'time of accountability' rather than a static point. The reasons for this unease are not hard to find.

First, common sense observation as well as scientific study suggests that *children undergo development in their ability to discern right and wrong* and in their capacity to make moral-cum-spiritual decisions. This would suggest that the notion of a fixed point at which a child becomes responsible must be abandoned. Instead we must begin to think of a series of points over time at which a child becomes increasingly responsible and therefore increasingly accountable.

> ## We must begin to think of a series of points over time at which a child becomes increasingly responsible and therefore increasingly accountable.

Secondly, although there are common patterns in child development, *children are amazingly varied in the speeds at which they develop.* If this is true, it becomes impossible to fix upon a single age common to *all* youngsters at which they become accountable. The age at which they do become so will vary with each child and will take account of a complex set of factors – mental, emotional, moral and spiritual, cultural and physical, the effects of nurture, experience and conditioning.

Thirdly, we can be helped in our thinking by *noticing what the law of the land makes of accountability.* In many ways, the question is similar both for the Christian trying to assess how far a child is accountable to God for acts of wrongdoing, and the legislator trying to draw up rules for determining when a child must be held accountable to human laws. It is significant that in Britain the law recognises rising degrees of responsibility for criminal actions between the ages of ten and seventeen. Only when a person reaches seventeen is he or she treated as an adult. Moreover, justice by common consent requires flexibility in punishment according to circumstances. Even though two children may commit identical crimes, their differences of background, motive and intention, have to be taken into account. In the end a magistrate may decide that one should be held more accountable than the other because he or she is able to exercise a greater degree of responsibility. So it is clear that the matter of accountability is a complex one and that the notion of a single fixed point applicable to all children in all circumstances at all times is an illusion.

If we apply these reflections to the theological realm, it would seem that we cannot hold to a simple idea of an age of accountability. Are we therefore reduced to saying that children should not be regarded as responsible at all?

It would be easy either to take this line uncritically or to advocate the opposite: that children are just as accountable as adults. I would argue, however, that both of these alternatives are unsatisfactory and that the third way, the concept of *developing accountability*, will enable us to take both sin and accountability seriously.

Pointers from theology

It is important to recognise one crucial theological fact: nowhere in scripture do we find biblical writers concerned with the questions which agitate us so greatly. They simply did not think in our categories and we will search in vain for a discussion of the destiny of non-adults.

If nothing else, this should make us wary of dogmatic conclusions. Paul's discussion of sin in Romans 1–5, for example (whether understood as a power or a state), says nothing about children. As we have seen, it is taken up with the status of the human race as a whole and even here the thought is of the adult race. As he declares that no one can claim to be righteous before God (Romans 3:23), Paul has nowhere in mind the question of children. The examples he uses to illustrate our wilful rebellion are all adult-centred: idolatry, sexual degradation, lust, murder, slander (1:18–31). 'God gave them over to a depraved mind' (1:28).

Now it is impossible to read into this a simple doctrine of child sin unless we are prepared, against the evidence of the text, to say that Paul *was* thinking of children as he wrote. But that is plainly beyond the scope of the passage: can we really believe that Paul is accusing children of sexual depravity, lust, murder and the rest? No, the most that we can say about the meaning of the text is that Paul was writing to make it clear that no one can claim righteousness on the basis of obedience to the law or any human standard. Such claims, of course, were adult in character.

To say this is not to deny the reality of inborn sinfulness. We are all offspring of Adam and this produces in us a desire for independence and self will which is the essence of sin. But again, we have to recognise that nowhere does Paul develop this thought in the context of children. His discussion in Romans 5 is designed to contrast the plight of man by nature with the salvation wrought by Christ. Although his arguments assume the reality of inborn sinfulness, if we are to be true to the text we have to acknowledge that Paul does not address the question of children, and that his concern is to show his (adult) readers the depth of what God has done in Christ.

We are left, then, with a major problem. The key biblical passages which address the questions of sin and salvation do not seem to be designed to answer our particular set of child-centred questions. Does this mean that the questions are invalid or unanswerable? Must we simply accept that we can say nothing about how the great Christian doctrines apply to children?

The key biblical passages which address the questions of sin and salvation do not seem to be designed to answer our particular set of child-centred questions.

Fortunately not. The Bible does contain some clues but they are nowhere as clear or systematic as some writers have suggested or as we might wish.

Christian households

The first clue lies in Paul's admonitions to Christian households. In Colossians 3:20 he exhorts children to obey their parents 'for this pleases the Lord'. The implication is that disobedience will displease the Lord and thereby constitute sin. Similarly, in Ephesians children are commanded to obey their parents 'in the Lord' because this is right and because it will bring blessing from God. Not to do so would be a transgression. To underline the point, Paul cites the commandment, 'Honour your father and mother'.

It is clear that from these passages that *children could and did sin*. The principle of inborn sinfulness did not simply come into play at adulthood. But beyond the *fact* of child sinfulness neither Paul nor the other New Testament writers were prepared to go.

Jesus and children

The second clue lies in Jesus' attitude to children. There are a number of passages in the Gospels which feature Jesus and children. These are not always straightforward and we must beware of reading our own meanings back into the texts. However, examination of Mark 9:36 and 37 reveals three aspects of Jesus' attitude to children:

> 'And he took a child and put him in the midst of them; and
> taking him in his arms, he said to them, "Whoever receives
> one such child in my name receives me; and whoever
> receives me, receives not me but him who sent me."'(RSV)

First, we see that *Jesus commends children to our loving care.* In the New Testament the expression 'to receive somebody' always indicates warm and open hospitality. Moreover, in the Jewish environment, this idea included adoption of orphans into the family as if they were one of the family's own. By literally opening his arms to a child, therefore, Jesus was demonstrating the kind of love God expects us to show towards children.

Second, *Jesus points to a special relationship.* 'Whoever receives one such child in my name ...' Behind this formula lies a very powerful idea. In Semitic thought, a king would send his representative to act on his behalf bearing the formula 'in my name'. The representative was to be seen as having as much importance as the king himself. As one rabbi put it, 'the envoy of the king is as the king himself.' Jesus, in effect, is declaring a child to be the envoy of God!

Such a thought must have seemed shocking to the disciples. We know from the next chapter that they tried to send the children away (Mark 10:13–15). But Jesus affirmed his (and therefore his Father's) special relationship with them by forbidding the disciples to dismiss them, and by blessing them.

Third, *the presence of the children signified the presence of the kingdom* (Mark 10:16). This is an extension of the previous idea. If the children are representatives of God, then God's kingdom must be present. Jesus does not explain in detail how this is the case but the biblical scholar Hans-Ruedi Weber sums it up thus:

> 'It is the relationship with Jesus which makes these children

representatives of God. As such they are our teachers. In their objective humility and need, they cry "mother", "father", "Abba", and they stretch out their empty hands. If we want to learn how to become God's representatives, we must learn it from the child in our midst.'[3]

The attitude of Jesus to children, therefore, unlike the general attitude of his day, was to welcome and accept children as loved by God and as metaphors of God's presence. This gives positive and biblical reinforcement to our belief that the atoning love of God covers children – a theme to which we shall return later in this chapter and the next.

Insights from child development

It will already be apparent that I believe the best way of understanding accountability is in terms of development. There is no single point at which children universally, or individually, suddenly become accountable: each moves through an increasing degree of accountability until he or she reaches full responsibility in adulthood. This seems to fit most readily with what we have noted about the biblical categories of sin and salvation.

The strength of this approach is that it takes seriously the models of development we have already examined in part one. In pre-modern times, children were regarded from many points of view as mini-adults. Family organisation in pre-industrial England assumed that as soon as they could fulfil basic physical tasks, children should play their part in the economy of the household. So it was that they worked in the fields, and later, in the factories of the Industrial Revolution. They were expected to behave like adults. Examples of this today can be seen in some African societies where the Western ethos has not taken hold.

Children in Western societies, however, are separated from the adult world at a very early age by school and pre-school institutions designed to reinforce childhood as a distinct phase of development in its own right. We do not recognise that adulthood has been attained until they reach eighteen. The fact that some societies draw the line differently shows how relative the notion of an age of accountability is.

In order to develop a framework of spiritual accountability, therefore, we need to find a model or combination of models of child development which will address the kind of questions we face when asking what it means to be responsible before God. These can be found by comparing the faith models offered by Fowler and Westerhoff, with research carried out in the field of *personal moral development.* Here questions about the development of children's attitudes to right and wrong parallel theological questions about their understanding of sin.

Many contemporary researchers in child development, inspired by the work of educationalists Jean Piaget and Lawrence Kohlberg, indicate the processes of change which take place in children as their cognitive capacities and moral awareness develop. Though not all would now follow them in detail, the proposed stages still indicate the directions of much research and we do not have to accept them uncritically to appreciate that there is much to learn from the basic tenets of their work.[4] The models we shall look at below should not therefore be taken as 'gospel' but as working theories to help us understand more about child development. Like all models, they remain open to debate and modification.

Moral development

Building on the work of Piaget, Lawrence Kohlberg developed a sophisticated model based on six stages, grouped in three sets of two:

A. The pre-moral level
Stage 1: The child defines right and wrong by whether an action brings punishment. Rightness is not a matter of doing right according to some underlying moral order but simply avoiding punishment.

Stage 2: The right thing to do is what brings reward. Other people are not valuable in themselves but as instruments for getting what we want.

B. The conventional level
Stage 3: The child conforms to standards of right and wrong for fear of disapproval by others, especially adults. Kohlberg calls this the 'Good Boy-Nice Girl' stage. (Many adults' attitudes toward God are stuck at this level.)

Stage 4: Right is defined by obedience to authority. Rules are to be obeyed because they are right in themselves, irrespective of their content. So if a teacher concocts a game which has an element of injustice in it, it is always right to obey the teacher even though this may involve injustice.

C. The principled level

Stage 5: Morality is a matter of sticking to generally agreed rules. These are seen as necessary to protect individual rights. They can be changed by social agreement but individuals are not free to break them at will. Thus the rules of a game may be changed provided everyone agrees but one player alone may not act outside the rules for his or her own benefit.

Stage 6: Right and wrong are defined by a person freely choosing standards and principles for him or herself. Morality is not a matter of living up to others' expectations but of making up one's own mind. Personal rules should, however, respect the just rights of others and not be merely self-serving.

If we accept the basic direction of this model, it seems clear that the growth of adult moral capacity is a lengthy and complex process. Although, since his original work, Kohlberg has modified his model to recognise that few people ever reach the fullness of stage six, adult moral responsibility is nevertheless reckoned in terms of:

1. Awareness of the rights of others.
2. Ability to accept obligations arising from abstract values.
3. Willingness to forgo self-centredness.
4. Making up one's own mind.

Conclusions drawn from the development model

How does this model help us in our theological understanding of accountability?

1. The first and most important insight it offers is to provide *confirmation that responsibility and therefore accountability should be seen in terms of development.* The degree to which children should be held responsible for their actions must reflect the stage they have reached along the developmental line.

In practical terms, this will mean that we will not seek to hold children accountable for a stage of moral capacity they have not yet reached. A junior child, for example, can be held responsible for his attitude to concrete rules which govern specific kinds of situations but it may not be appropriate to expect him to reason in terms of abstract values. We could rightly expect obedience, for example, to the rule 'do not steal from shops', or 'do not hit your sister to get her sweets'. These are both specific and concrete. But we could not fairly expect a child to translate into practice such abstract principles as, 'honesty is a good thing' or 'violence and covetousness are wrong'. Accountability for failing to live up to abstractions must await adolescence. (It is perhaps no coincidence that the biblical command to obey one's parents is a very concrete moral instruction.)

2. It follows that *it would be unjust to condemn a child for not living up to a law of God designed to be fulfilled by adults.* We cannot expect children in stages one and two of Kohlberg's model to live as if they were in stages five or six. To do so is unjust and unrealistic. It is the moral equivalent of expecting an infant who had just learned to count to solve differential equations.

These insights will affect the way we approach the themes of sin and atonement. If we are wise we will not assume that adult-oriented categories can be applied in a straightforward way to children. When we speak of them as sinners, we shall be careful to think of sin in appropriate terms: we shall not make the mistake of confusing biblical texts directed at adults with the spiritual status of children. We shall certainly not assume that the heart of a child is simply the heart of an adult in a smaller body.

To tell a child that sin is breaking God's law will not mean much. Telling him that sin is stealing someone's sweets or bashing his enemy in the playground will carry the message home.

On the other hand, we shall not avoid the question of accountability by assuming that children are free from sin altogether. That is not the proper inference to be drawn either from Paul or from the study of development. The issue is not whether children are accountable or not, but *what kind* of accountability is appropriate. As I have tried to show, we should hold a child responsible only at the level which he has reached. To do otherwise would be to deny both God's justice and his love.

A revised model for sin and accountability

If we bring together all the models of development we have so far discussed, one fact is clear: sin means something radically different to a child of three from what it means to a child of fifteen. It is not just that some sins seem childish and others adult; the two children have vastly different capacities to comprehend the idea of sin. This seems common sense but, as we have seen, evangelists have not always recognised it either theologically or practically.

Once we accept that the meaning of sin varies from one stage of development to another, it follows that the meaning of accountability must vary likewise.

The infant stage
Children operate entirely at the instinctive, discovery level. The ingredients of moral or spiritual understanding are undeveloped.

The late infant/early junior stage
Young children are learning to test limits even further. They know what it means to say 'no' and to disobey. Wilful identity is starting to develop but right and wrong are still defined by what parents say. If 'sin' has any meaning at all, it is in terms of disobeying parents. But even here the intellectual dimension of sin is missing. The decision to disobey is not based on a knowledge of what is right and wrong, or on being able to work out what they mean in practice. It is not a rational decision at all.

The junior stage
Growing children define right and wrong in terms of obeying (a) their group of friends and their code, and (b) rules and commands imposed by adults. Their understanding of sin is more complex but they conceive of

it in concrete terms. They must still be held responsible for acts of disobedience but this understanding is limited by their mental apparatus which is geared to concrete ways of thinking.

Theologically, therefore, sin for the child means definite, specific, concrete actions. Abstract concepts such as lovelessness or injustice are meaningless without concrete examples within the scope of the child's experience. To tell a child that sin is breaking God's law will not mean much. Telling him that sin is stealing someone's sweets or bashing his enemy in the playground will carry the message home.

At this stage, also, the idea of sin as an offence against God as a person who is distinct from parents begins to take shape. Although right and wrong have been associated primarily with commands issued by tangible, visible human adults, children in junior years increasingly become aware of God as a being distinct from Mum or Dad, who lays down a code of right and wrong which even adults must obey!

The adolescent stage

The child's increasing ability to handle abstract concepts and to move from concrete, specific instances of wrongdoing to general rules about right and wrong means that he is close to being able to understand fully biblical teaching on sin. There is a growing awareness of sin as something which brings pain to God because it undermines the basis of covenant love. Sin thus becomes not simply a matter of breaking rules but of destroying a relationship. Although junior children may be able to glimpse something of this, it is only the flowering during adolescence of the ability to really take another person's perspective (empathy) that allows a child to grasp the full meaning of sin – that it is a heartbreaking experience for God which can be dealt with only through the heartbreaking suffering love of the Son of God.

During this stage, therefore, it becomes possible to speak of sin both as a breaking of universal divine laws and as a disruption of the relationship of love between God and man. Since the child's understanding of justice is also developing at this time, the idea of sin as an injustice towards God may carry real meaning.

Where does this leave us in relation to accountability? We shall visit the question of children from believing homes in chapter seven but in my view, the balance of the argument lies with the view that all children are included within the atoning work of Christ until they reject him. Given what we know about stages of faith and child development, it is both unjust and unrealistic to think that children below adolescence should be held responsible for sin viewed from an adult perspective. Moreover, our theology of God and God's character means that while we must recognise that he does not take sin lightly (hence the atonement), his love and justice rule out the idea of holding a person accountable for that which he can neither understand nor fulfil.

In the contemporary world, this point is even more important than in previous generations. Increasingly, children come from homes in which God is never mentioned at all (except perhaps as a swear-word) and in which the gospel is conspicuous by its absence. The alternative to regarding all children as covered by the gracious atoning work of Christ on the cross until they refuse him, is to regard them as condemned. This may have been a position taken by an earlier generation of evangelists but it is one I would find hard to square with a biblical picture in which God's justice is interpreted by his love (thus the cross) and in which Jesus goes out of his way (unsentimentally, it should be noted) to *include* children.

This is not to say that sin does not matter or that it is not real prior to adolescence. Far from it. But its meaning is significantly different. A baby in the shopping trolley who takes sweets from the shelf at the supermarket and then eats them on the spot may be doing something undesirable (at least from the mother's point of view). But the twelve year old who deliberately does the same thing with the intention of avoiding payment is in a different category altogether. We would not dream of judging the two identically; and so it is with sin and accountability. When we reach the stage of intentionally, wilfully and repeatedly refusing God, then we have entered into the fullness of sin and God will reckon us wholly accountable. The atonement may cover those who do not fully understand what it means to break God's heart or do not know they are doing it, but for those who know and delight in sin, there must either be repentance, forgiveness and renewal or, ultimately, condemnation. But until such time as a child is able to understand and consciously *reject* Christ, we must assume that the love, mercy and justice of God are met in the atoning work of his suffering, servant Son. If the gospel means anything, it surely means this.

Conclusion

The argument of the last chapter can be summed up as follows:

1. There is no necessary conflict between developmental and theological accounts of human sinfulness. They can be integrated at a number of crucial points.
2. Both psychology and scripture affirm the reality and power of self-centredness which lies at the heart of sin, although scripture introduces the key aspect of sin in our relationship toward God.
3. A child's understanding of the meaning of sin is relative to the stage of moral, emotional, educational and spiritual development he has reached.
4. The notion of accountability must likewise relate to stages of growth. It is better to speak of a continuum of accountability rather than a moment or age of accountability.
5. It is unjust to impose on children definitions of sin and accountability which presuppose adult capacities.
6. God's love, mercy and justice require that we do not speculate about the judgement of God further than scripture allows. Given all the considerations above, this means we shall include children within the atonement.

Notes to chapter 6

1   Ron Buckland, *Children and the King*, Surrey Hills, Anzea, 1979, p68.
2   John Inchley, *All About Children*, Eastbourne, Coverdale, 1976, p130.
3   Hans Reudi Weber, *Jesus and the Children*, Geneva, WCC 1979, p51.
4   Margaret Donaldson in *Children's Minds* (Fontana, 1978) has taken issue with Piaget and Kohlberg. She maintains that a child's perception of right and wrong has less to do with age than with the context in which he or she is introduced to notions of right aand wrong. On this argument even a young child can understand basic rules and the need to obey them. This is a useful insight to have alongside Piaget and Kohlberg and reminds us that their framework must not be taken inflexibly.

7 Faith development and conversion

The faith status of children

Having worked through part one of this book, the reader could be forgiven for asking the following question: 'If faith development is a natural and inevitable process, where does the idea of conversion fit in?'

Traditional evangelical assumptions

Among those who work evangelistically with children there often still exists the presumption that conversion is concerned with an event or moment in the life of an individual child, when he or she makes a decision to turn to Christ and to accept him. On this view, a children's mission would be geared up to a message which contains some or all of the following elements: (a) God the Creator; (b) humans as sinners; (c) Jesus the Saviour; (d) our need to respond; (e) Jesus the friend. A standard five-day mission might climax on the fourth or fifth day with a call to repentance, faith and a conscious decision to follow Christ.

At this point, it is important to understand what is *not* being said. I am not saying that every mission or event follows this pattern rigidly. Many will major on some aspect of Jesus' life rather than on a series of theological themes. But somewhere along the line these themes will emerge in some shape or form: certainly (b), (c) and (d) will for they constitute the core of the gospel and it would be hard to imagine evangelism which did not contain them.

Neither am I saying that this structure is all bad. It is clearly not: God has used and blessed it for many years and I myself have led holiday missions based upon it.

However, if we are committed to child evangelism we must now ask what we can learn from the study of child development which will help us in our goal of bringing Christ to all ages. In particular we need to ask whether our model of conversion is not too adult and simplistic. For the structure of our evangelistic teaching remains specifically designed to evoke a response of faith which is (adult) decision-centred. This is why so much of a typical week's mission programme is geared to preparing children to hear about the atonement on day four or five: we hope that by first setting the scene for the cross (the fact of sin, our need of forgiveness, etc) in days one to three, and then by emphasising the awfulness and costliness of Calvary, we will evoke a decision, on the part of the child listener, to accept Christ.

We need to ask whether our model of conversion is not too adult and simplistic.

However, alongside the idea of conversion as an *event* we need to set the model of conversion as a *process*. Merely because someone is unable to name the day they were converted, or trace the experience to a specific moment does not mean they are any the less converted. For children and adults alike, conversion may take place as a process over a period of time rather than at a definite point in time. The Spirit of God can be seen at work in both instances. It is important to hold the event and process models together.

What is conversion?

We can approach this question from two directions. *Theologically*, we can ask what the Bible means by conversion and how this relates to the work of the Father, Son and Spirit. *Developmentally*, we can ask how the processes of child and faith development we have noted in part one of this book fit with a theological understanding of conversion. In the remainder of this chapter we shall look at both of these. We will begin by looking at the developmental views of faith and conversion: of John Westerhoff and James Fowler. In addition, we shall consider the implications of the work of James Loder, whose discussion of the notion of transformation has brought further insight into what it means to be converted.

Development models and conversion

John Westerhoff: Faith Stages

John Westerhoff, writing from the perspective of what conversion means for someone who has grown up within the Christian faith, describes it as 'radical turning from "faith given" (through nurture) to "faith owned".[1] In this he draws his model of the fourfold sequence of faith development which we noted earlier: *experienced* (or given) faith, *affiliative* faith, *searching* faith and *owned* faith. Conversion comes as the bridge between stages three and four and is the 'act of surrender' by which a person gives him or herself wholly to God in a new and life-changing way. The entire process may take a substantial period of time or may be compressed into a short space of time. For Westerhoff, conversion is both process *and* moment in that the process leads to a moment when the individual commits to owned faith. Two passages make this clear:

> Conversion experiences may be sudden or gradual,
> dramatic or undramatic, emotional or intellectual, but they
> always involve a major change in a persons' thinking,
> feeling and willing - in short, in their total behaviour.[2]

> Conversion ... implies a reorientation in our thinking,
> feeling and willing; a moving from indifference or one
> form of piety to another. That is why conversion
> historically is rarely a singular emotional outburst, a once-
> for-all dramatic occasion which can be dated and described.
> Rather, conversion is more typically a process by which
> persons are nurtured in a community's faith (the religion of
> the heart), go through the despair of doubt and the
> intellectual quest for understanding (the religion of the
> head), and at last, in late adolescence or early adulthood,
> experience illumination, certainty and identity.[3]

John Westerhoff: Faith stages

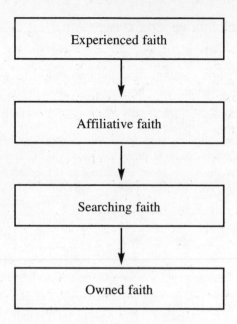

In Westerhoff's view, therefore, conversion is the outcome of both a moment and a process. The process of development comes to a head in the momentary act of surrender when the individual renounces self and gives everything to Christ. At that point she moves from faith given to her largely by others, to a faith which is appropriated and held for herself. '*The* faith' becomes '*her* faith'. She has reached the stage of owned faith.

Differences with the classical evangelical model

So far, this fits with the classic evangelical model of conversion. But there are significant differences.

1. Westerhoff insists that conversion can never be separated from

what has gone before. The life history of the convert is the soil out of which faith grows. The nurturing process of the preceding years is all important: 'Conversion ... is never an isolated event devoid of all elements of nurture. Nurture and conversion are a unified whole.'[4]

2. Westerhoff locates the point of conversion overwhelmingly in late adolescence or early adulthood. This is no accident. His developmental structure requires that the sequence of faith stages must be gone through before conversion can take place. By definition, the act of surrender must come as a result of dissatisfaction with former affiliative faith and the desire to find something personally meaningful. This cannot happen until adolescence at the earliest.[5]

Implications of Westerhoff's analysis

Whether we agree or not with Westerhoff's analysis (especially with his association of conversion with adolescence), it carries some radical implications for children's evangelism. The most serious of these is the question of whether we can rightly speak at all of conversion before adolescence. On Westerhoff's scheme, it would seem that we cannot, since true conversion presupposes searching and surrender which are characteristics of adolescence and adulthood rather than childhood. The kind of sequence which culminates in the intellectual despair and desperation described by Westerhoff is not part of the childhood phases of development in any sense. Neither intellectually nor emotionally is a pre-adolescent ready or capable of the reactions and responses involved in conversion as defined by the Westerhoff model.

At first sight, it might seem that Westerhoff is saying that it is impossible for pre-adolescents to enter into a real relationship with Jesus. But that would be too radical a reading of his model and certainly doesn't represent the view I am seeking to put forward in this book.

Rather, Westerhoff should be understood as arguing that adult models of conversion may be inappropriate for children, given the developmental processes at work in a child's life. The kind of commitment presupposed by the 'act of surrender' (for Westerhoff at least) is essentially adult and should not – on his reasoning – be imposed on children.

But this does not deny that pre-adolescents are capable of a relationship with Christ. There is abundant evidence, both from scripture and experience, that such relationships are not only possible but should be encouraged. It was children, after all, that Jesus actively sought out as symbols of the kingdom, and children whom he deliberately welcomed despite the scorn of the adult onlookers.

Consequently, I think on Westerhoff's logic, when we preach the gospel to children we are doing several things which might best be described as pre-conversional. Firstly, we are *sowing seed for the future.* Children who hear the gospel may not yet be ready for the act of surrender and the stage of owned faith but they can store away the truth for the time when it will become relevant. A ten year old child who attends a holiday mission may find that five or six years later, in the midst of her searching, she recalls what she learned about Jesus at the mission. Now it becomes real for the first time. The meaning for which she has been searching suddenly (or slowly) clicks into place. The seed has come to fruition.

> Children who hear the gospel may not yet be ready for the act of surrender and the stage of owned faith but they can store away the truth for the time when it will become relevant.

Secondly, we may be *persuading a child simply to switch her affiliation.* If we remind ourselves of the development models, we shall recall that juniorhood and early adolescence constitute a period of affiliation. Children adopt beliefs which are those of the crowd or other influential persons such as parents. It is unlikely, given what we know about the structure of child development, that a junior child who comes along to a mission or Sunday school will be converted in the sense of making an independent decision to reorientate her life in a fully adult way. This requires a more integral approach than children are generally capable of. What is much more likely is that the child who appears to make a decision for Christ at a mission, club or Sunday school has decided to start a new affiliation. This need not be a matter of insincerity: the desire to give his loyalty to a new group (the mission, church or whatever) can represent a genuinely heartfelt act. The giving of loyalty and the finding of meaning in a new group (particularly one which is not generally popular) is the central and greatest act of sincerity a child can make at this stage. It represents a powerful act of commitment.

But the meaning of such a commitment may lie in affiliation to the group, rather than to a personal acceptance of a set of truths. Sometimes this may include a powerful individual faith in the person of Jesus, sometimes a commitment to the shared faith of the group. We should not frown upon such group faith or regard it as inferior. Commitment to the group is often the highest form of commitment a child can make outside his or her immediate family relationships. We should not be looking for responses which are characteristically adult but for those which are realistically appropriate to child development.

This goes a long way to explaining two things common among children's missions and clubs. On one hand, there are frequently large numbers of children who make professions of faith or who want Jesus to be their friend; on the other hand there is often a high subsequent dropout rate. Children who were initially full of enthusiasm fall away. Those who have been faithful in attendance become less regular. Others are never seen at all between missions. (This is especially true of church-based missions which run every summer.) When this happens it is tempting to think that the child or children in question never really made a commitment of faith. 'If they were really disciples,' we say to ourselves, 'they would not have fallen away. Therefore they must never have been true Christians in the first place.'

The fact is that they probably never were – that is, *as long as being a true Christian is defined in terms of an adult conversion experience.* But my point is that this is the wrong standard by which to judge. The question is not whether they were ever genuinely converted but what kind of faith stage were/are they at? And whereabouts in the *process* of conversion are they? Many children who affiliate to a Christian group as a result of a mission move on to discover new affiliations after a time. This is not a deliberate renunciation of Christ: it is merely a part of the normal process of development. 'Taking Jesus as my friend', then, often means, 'Finding new friends who also want to join this group' (in which case the spiritual formula used by the evangelist to denote acceptance of Christ functions like the enrolment oath of Brownies or Girl Guides – it signifies acceptance into the new affiliation). Or it may mean, 'I accept as true the beliefs this group holds as important and want to join it.' (The problem with this is that it is hard to know what the notions of acceptance and belief mean to a child in this situation.) Or it may mean, 'I like what I have found in this group and the people who run it and am therefore prepared to do what they want in order to belong.' If this means saying a prayer of repentance and faith in Jesus, then unless the child is an outright atheist she will happily say a prayer. Again, we must not fall into the trap of supposing that it might not be genuine. The notion of hypocrisy is essentially adult. Within the framework of understanding and commitment which governs the affiliative stage, there will be very few children who (provided the cost of discipleship has been properly explained) will say they want to take Jesus as their friend if they do not mean it.

Thirdly, when we evangelise we may be *triggering a child's movement from one stage of faith to another.* The fourteen-year-old who hears the gospel may, for the first time in his life, be faced with the ultimate questions of life and death which lead on to the searching stage. But this will not always be so. It is not easy to trigger ultimate questions when a group is comfortably off and has never experienced hardship or grief. Such is the nature of modern life that many teenagers are able to coast along on the cushion of prosperity and security afforded by the culture of contentment. Many others, however, are experiencing the harsh side of this economic climate, and grow up with insecurity as a part of daily life. Nevertheless, when the questioning, searching stage is reached (and this may not be till the twenties or thirties), a person who has heard the gospel as a teenager or child will frequently find herself going back to what she heard years before.

We need to be clear, finally, that each of the stages described by Westerhoff is a stage of *faith*. It is not a question of a child's suddenly reaching faith at the final stage. All the way through, faith has been at work. As Westerhoff says: 'Let us never forget that ... Christ died for us all, and no matter what style of faith we possess none are outside his redeeming grace.'[6]

Our evangelism ... must be geared to
enabling a child to expand such faith as
he or she possesses.

Our evangelism, therefore, must be geared to enabling a child to *expand* such faith as he or she possesses.

Does this mean that we can never talk meaningfully about the conversion of children? To answer this we must turn to another developmental model.

James Fowler: Faith content and conversion

James Fowler, while accepting Westerhoff's four stages of faith, offers a definition of conversion which is not confined to adolescence or adulthood. In his view, 'Conversion has to do with changes in the *contents* of faith.'[7] This can take place at any stage of development since there will always be some content to a child's faith (at least after infancy). It does not have to follow a period of searching or despair.

Fowler is able to adopt this definition of conversion because he originally defines faith as a set of meanings by which we give order and sense to our lives. It follows that we can change this set of meanings at any point and do not have to wait till adolescence or adulthood to do so. A child, for example, who has not been brought up to believe in Jesus may attend a mission or club in which the Christian faith clearly makes sense to the people who run it, whom he likes, and which therefore begins to make sense to him. As a result, he may decide to incorporate some of their beliefs and symbols into his own life. Time alone will tell whether these come to occupy the dominant place in his way of thinking but the point is that it is possible in principle that they will do so, even prior to adolescence.

On this basis, the goal of evangelism must be to enable a child to accept a new set of meanings based on the idea of a relationship with Christ. These do not have to be understood in adult terms. The set of meanings can be geared to the appropriate stage of development so as to take account of the factors discussed in part one. In speaking to junior age children, for example, we shall be concerned to couch this new set of meanings in concrete terms. In younger groups we might major on the idea of God as loving parent and so on.

According to Fowler, then, a person can be converted at any stage of life or faith. It is the change of content that matters rather than the stage of faith that has been reached. However, in addition to conversion thus defined, Fowler identifies two other experiences commonly thought of as conversion but which (he maintains) should not be counted as such because they do not involve a change of content.[8]

The first of these he terms an intensification experience. This is a rather jargonistic way of describing an experience which deepens or renews previously held faith but which does not affect its contents. It amounts to an intense version of what has already been experienced. An example of this would be the adult who once was a fervent Christian but who has drifted away. He has not lost his faith but has become slack. He attends a church meeting and is renewed in faith and commitment. What has happened is not conversion since he has not discovered a new content of faith: he has merely come back to his first love with renewed intensity.

The second experience does not have a convenient label. It involves being *catapulted from one faith stage to another by an event or experience*. But it does not involve any change in basic meanings or content. The movement, even though dramatic or sudden, takes place within the stream of faith in which the person was already situated. Thus a man who is stuck in the affiliative stage might be brought into the reflective stage by a tragedy within the family, such as the death of his wife. As he reflects upon the meaning of death he realises that his previous shallow views are no longer adequate and begins to search for a deeper faith which will enable him to cope. Merely parroting the views of others ('She's at peace now. She can't suffer any more.') is not enough. He has to find a set of meanings which will make sense of what has happened. He does so by moving on to the reflective stage within his previous tradition of belief. Hopefully, if he has been within the context of Christian nurture, he does not switch to Buddhism to provide the answer to his questions but goes more deeply into Christian teaching about the resurrection. This is but one example.

Fowler's five ways

From these three experiences – conversion, intensification and movement from one stage to another – Fowler argues that we can trace five ways in which conversion relates to stages of faith:

1. *Stage change without conversion,* as in the example above of the bereaved husband.
2. *Stage change that triggers conversion.* An example of this would be an adolescent who is in the affiliative stage but who begins to ask questions of meaning and purpose and in the process of moving into the reflective stage finds Christ at an evangelistic rally.

James Fowler: Faith content

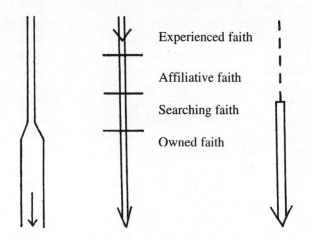

Experienced faith

Affiliative faith

Searching faith

Owned faith

FAITH
INTENSIFICATION

MOVEMENT FROM ONE
STAGE TO ANOTHER

CONVERSION

3. *Conversion without stage change,* as in the case of an eleven-year-old from a humanist background who embraces the Christian faith but who remains at the affiliative stage.

4. *Conversion that triggers stage change.* Suppose the teenager above goes forward at a rally with his mates. None of them has a Christian background. Along with them, he changes the content of his faith but is still at the affiliative stage. But now suppose that this leads to his becoming more reflective as he reads the Bible and realises that he has to commit his life fully to Christ. His conversion has triggered off a stage change.

5. *Conversion followed by blocked stage change.* An example of this would be someone converted to Christ at a children's camp or mission who never grew in maturity of faith as he or she got older. Such a person

might hold a sincere and deeply felt faith but it would remain essentially as naive and undeveloped as at conversion. When confronted by doubt or questioning it either retreats into itself or collapses. Unfortunately, there are many such Christians in today's churches.

Conversion, then, is no simple matter. On Fowler's model, conversion does not refer so much to a sudden, dramatic experience as to a change in the meanings by which we order our lives, whether these come from faith in Christ or some other creed or commitment. This may involve a single, powerful experience or it may not.

Integration

One school of thought rules out child conversion whereas another would seem to rule it in. The Bible however makes it clear that children of any age can have a meaningful relationship with Jesus.

This divergence may not be as serious as first sight suggests. If we compare Westerhoff and Fowler, we see that Westerhoff stresses the *attitude* of conversion while Fowler stresses the *content*. These need not be mutually exclusive. The content of Christian conversion must be faith in Christ. The adult or child who seeks Jesus must come to the point of giving himself or herself into his hands and asking Christ to rule his life. Westerhoff (I think) would be uneasy with this in the case of children because the searching phase which precedes the act of surrender presupposes characteristics that lie beyond childhood. Fowler, on the other hand, does not lay so much emphasis upon surrender and therefore can incorporate conversion within early stages of faith.

The answer may lie in broadening the notion of surrender to take into account the characteristics of childhood. While it may be true that children do not have the capacity to go through the reflection and doubt at the heart of the searching stage, they nevertheless are capable of giving themselves to Jesus within the limits set by affiliative faith. The ten-year-old who enjoys a mission and wants to join the Jesus gang may still grasp that she is taking a step of commitment. Good evangelism will always make clear that becoming a friend of Jesus means giving everything over to him. Even if the child interprets this to mean that she must trust and obey the leaders of the Jesus gang, this still represents an act of surrender.

We must accept that both Fowler and Westerhoff offer valuable insights into conversion and that whilst there are some differences between them, we are best served by incorporating insights from both. However, it is at this point that the work of another theologian, psychologist and theorist of religious education can help.

James Loder

In his book *The Transforming Moment*, Loder puts forward a model based on five steps. As we shall see, it is similar in many ways to the kind of thinking contained within Westerhoff and Fowler. But there is one important difference: the role Loder attaches to the power of imagination. This is highly significant given all we have noted earlier about the centrality of imagination to faith development, and it is for this reason that Loder's model is included here.

In step one, Loder identifies 'conflict' as the key characteristic. A new experience, thought or idea disturbs the equilibrium of the individual, giving rise to a sense of unease or disturbance. The individual's previous feeling that 'everything's okay' is in some way ruptured. The content of the experience or thought is not the key issue: the fact that it disturbs the individual's equilibrium is.

The second step, therefore, amounts to a pause while the person tries to resolve the disequilibrium. Loder calls this the 'interlude for scanning'. It is essentially an activity that takes place at the level of emotions and the subconscious. It is not an intellectual exercise. As one writer puts it, while it is taking place (possibly over a period of time rather than in an instant), 'the mind is asleep but the soul is awake'.

In the third step, the imagination comes into play. A possible resolution of the conflict appears not out of the processes of intellectual analysis and discussion but in the form of an *imaginative insight* or intuition. This supplies the key to understanding and dealing with the source of the disequilibrium. The fragments of the disturbance are brought together in a new whole so that the situation is seen in a fresh light and a way forward appears. Imagination is all-important at this stage.

Step four provides a 'release and opening' as the troubled person discovers the conflict is now resolved (or on the way to being resolved). The energy previously devoted to worrying about the problem or 'scanning' for a resolution is now released to achieve something positive. This 'something' is a new sense of knowing, a new trust and a new grasp of meaning. In other words, a renewed faith.

The fifth step is described by Loder as 'interpretation'. By this he means that the solution provided by the imagination moves from the realm of mind and feeling into behaviour. The inner sense of restored equilibrium must connect with the outer world. The individual must put his or her new way of seeing things into practice in daily life. It is no good simply feeling subjectively that a problem has been resolved: the resolution must affect real life. In biblical language, it must bear fruit.

This, then, is Loder's model of conversion. It clearly bears resemblances to Westerhoff and Fowler. But it is worth consideration in its own right for two reasons:

- Firstly, its emphasis on the importance of imagination sets it apart from the tendency (especially in Fowler) to see conversion largely in terms of the reasoning process. Loder's valuable insight is that because faith (as we have seen in part one) is a matter of the imagination as well as the mind, imagination has a key role in moving a person through the stages of conversion. The resolution of conflict (Westerhoff's movement from searching faith to owned faith, or Fowler's switches in the contents of faith) is brought about not so much by reasoned argument or persuasion but by an imaginative leap as the individual discovers an insight or image that suddenly or gradually makes new sense of the situation. Loder's rediscovery of the power of intuition and imagination is crucial.

- Secondly, Loder rightly stresses that conversion is never just about internal change. It must connect with the outside world. A person's life must show evidence of change, of the new reality taking hold. This chimes closely with the biblical emphasis on works as the fruit of faith and, moreover, properly underlines the fact that the individual must take his or her place within the community of faith that lives by love. In doing so, it demonstrates that conversion to Christ has real effects on others and not simply on the person who has undergone a conversion experience.

For these reasons, then, I have included the work of James Loder as helping us further understand the phenomenon of conversion. A hypothetical example will perhaps illustrate his model by way of conclusion.

Imagine Lee at fourteen years of age. It's a perilous period in his life for he has recently become a teenager with all that that entails.

Nonetheless, he thinks he has his life sorted out and is (in Loder's terms) in a state of equilibrium. Then something shattering happens: his sister is killed in a car accident. Nothing could be more destructive of his sense of well-being. He has entered the first stage of Loder's model.

In the next weeks and months, Lee is distraught and bereft. Nothing can make up for the loss. He is in turmoil but at the same time desperately wants the pain to diminish and to be able to make sense, emotionally as well as intellectually, of what has happened. At the subconscious level he is 'scanning' for a resolution.

Then one day he hears on the radio an interview with a young woman whose father was murdered the previous year. It is obvious she is religious for she talks about God having helped her through her grief. Lee thinks this is just words until she gets to the part where she talks about God's heart being broken. This is an image he has never considered before. He continues to listen carefully as she speaks of Jesus' dying on the cross and of God sharing his pain for the sin and suffering of the world. Finally, she uses the image of Christ suffering alongside – and entering into the pain of – the two other men upon crosses next to him and how that symbolises his suffering for the whole of humanity.

The image captures Lee's imagination; for although he knew the crucifixion story in outline, he had never thought of it in this way. Maybe, far from being the distant figure of history that Lee had previously considered him to be, Jesus is more than that. Maybe, his death offers a way of coming to terms with Lee's sister's death. The *image* of the suffering Christ opens up a new way of feeling and thinking which moves Lee forward emotionally and intellectually.

As Lee reflects upon the image of Christ's suffering love, it begins to take hold. It leads him to read the biblical accounts of the crucifixion. It dawns on him how much Jesus must have loved the world. Moreover, his reading of the crucifixion stories takes Lee inevitably onto the resurrection, which in turn opens new doors of imagination and insight. He is liberated into stage four as he starts to see reality – including his own life – in a revolutionary way. The combination of images of Jesus' death and rising to life also enables him to make sense (insofar as it is possible) of even his sister's death.

Lee is consequently well on the way to holistic conversion. His movement into stage five completes the process as he shares his experience with friends and family. At first they think he is simply taking refuge in religion as a way of coping with the pain of his grief. But as it becomes clear his entire way of thinking and behaving is undergoing change, they find themselves wondering, particularly as Lee feels compelled to join a church where he can find support and nourishment of his new-found faith.

This example, though more dramatic and clear-cut than would probably be the case in real life, nonetheless serves to illustrate how Loder's insights into the importance of imagination are valuable. They add to the models supplied by Westerhoff and Fowler so that taken in conjunction, all three give us a framework for understanding how faith development and conversion relate to one another. This is important if we are to take both seriously in the task of evangelism among children and young people.

It is impossible, however, to consider conversion solely in terms of developmental models. Conversion is a *theological* term and must be analysed theologically. Our next stop, therefore, will be the New Testament.

The New Testament and conversion

What does the New Testament mean by conversion? We can approach this in two ways. The first is to examine the terminology used by New Testament writers to speak of conversion. The second is to look at some key examples of conversion from the experience of the first Christians. As we do both of these we shall begin to see how theology and models of development can meet.

'Turning away'

The most common Greek word for conversion is *epistrepho*. Literally translated it means 'turning' or 'turning away'. Employed by the writers of the New Testament it takes on a threefold theological significance:

Firstly, it signifies a *'fundamental turning of the human will to God, a return home from blindness and error to the Saviour of all'*. It is not simply a matter of being sorry for the old way of life but a deliberate and heartfelt determination to change. Moreover, it is a recognition that such change can come about only by wholeheartedly turning to Christ. The person who is genuinely converted acknowledges that she cannot serve God by herself; her human will can always be bent by temptation and sin.

Only by a surrender to Christ and a life lived in the power of grace can a convert find a true turnaround.

Secondly, *epistrepho* points to a *change in lordship*. Before conversion, human beings are under the temporary lordship of Satan (Ephesians 2:1,2). Without realising it we follow his ways, live according to his dictates and are controlled by his power. We are in his kingdom of darkness whether we like it or not. But in Christ, God has triumphed over Satan. When we are converted we find a new Lord – Jesus Christ – who grants us perfect freedom within his kingdom of light. Conversion therefore means a total change in allegiance.

Thirdly, *epistrepho* indicates *a complete transformation of life in all respects*. Conversion does not lead to a chipping away at the edges of the former sinful self but to a radical remaking of every dimension. This is only possible in the power of the Holy Spirit. Left to ourselves we might long for radical change but only the Spirit can achieve such a transformation. Conversion is both brought about and sustained by God's Spirit. It is a supernatural work.

> Conversion does not lead to a chipping away at the edges of the former sinful self but to a radical remaking of every dimension.

Theologically, then, conversion is God's act from beginning to end. This may seem to conflict with the emphasis of faith development models but in reality it does not. For God's grace flows both through natural (God-created) channels *and* through the momentary intervention of the Holy Spirit. We can therefore say that the development of faith through stages over time and the immediate crisis of conversion arise from the same source – the living God.

Examples from the first Christians

When we turn to the experience of conversion among the first believers, we find the same process at work. The book of Acts records five incidents of individual conversions:

1. Paul: Acts 9 (see also Galatians 1 and Romans 7).
2. The Ethiopian eunuch: Acts 8.
3. Cornelius: Acts 10.
4. Lydia: Acts 16.
5. The Philippian jailer: Acts 16.

Although examination reveals that each of these conversions was unique, a certain pattern emerges:

The role of scripture

The first and most important element in this is the *role of scripture* in preparing a convert or evoking a sense of need. Paul is the most obvious case since he had been well versed in the law and the prophets as a Pharisee. But he was blind to their true meaning with regard to Christ. Once he had encountered the risen Lord, however, his knowledge was revolutionised. Under the creative inspiration of the Spirit, he was able to build a Christ-centred theology on the foundation of his deep knowledge of the Old Testament.

The Scriptures were also vital for the others. The Ethiopian eunuch had been reading and meditating on Isaiah 53 when Philip appeared. Philip's exposition of how Jesus fulfilled the role of suffering servant opened his eyes and he was converted. As far as Cornelius is concerned, Luke makes it clear that 'he and all his family were devout and God-fearing'. It is quite likely that this involved some awareness of the Old Testament. Certainly Peter in Acts 10:42 was preaching the gospel. In Lydia's case, her scriptural knowledge seems to have derived from the apostles, although she may have had some prior awareness. Luke records that when Paul and the others visited Philippi, they spoke with her and other devout women at a place of worship by the river. Given what we know from elsewhere about Paul's expositions of scripture in similar situations, we can deduce that the Scriptures had a definite role in triggering Lydia's conversion and may well have been influential before. This leaves us with the jailer. There is no indication about his level of scriptural awareness prior to his conversion but from the account in Acts 16 we do know that following the earthquake Paul and Silas 'spoke the word of the Lord to him and all that were in his house'. We can therefore discern a pattern in these five conversions which includes a pivotal role for the Scriptures.

The work of the Holy Spirit

The second factor is the *work of the Holy Spirit*. Paul is not explicit about the role of the Spirit in his conversion but it is implicit in his statement that God 'was pleased to reveal his Son' to him (Galatians 1:16). Since we know that the Spirit is God's chosen agent of revelation, it follows that what Paul is describing is the work of the Spirit. In the Ethiopian's case, however, the entire incident is explicitly surrounded by the Spirit: Philip is told by the Spirit to join the eunuch. The man then sees the truth and is baptised. Finally, Philip is taken away by the Spirit. The role of the Spirit could hardly be more pronounced. Cornelius' experience is different yet again. His conversion is accompanied by the gift of the Spirit and speaking in tongues (Acts 10:44–46). This should not be taken as a definitive sequence for all conversions since its purpose was to show that both conversion and the Holy Spirit were for the Gentiles as well as the Jews (see Acts 11). Nevertheless, it is clear that God was demonstrating that conversion must not be regarded as an act of the human will but had to be understood as something which could only take place under the impulse of the Spirit.

A preceding period of questioning

A third element we must notice is that in all but one case (the jailer), *the crisis of conversion was preceded by a period of questioning, inquiry or doubt*. Paul's experience on the road to Damascus seems to have come at the end of a time of inner conflict in which he had instigated the stoning of Stephen and had renewed his onslaught upon the Christians. It might be thought that these were signs of determination rather than conflict, but Paul's fanaticism betrayed the classic characteristics of insecurity and fear. This is reflected in his account of Jesus' words to him on the road: 'Saul, Saul, why do you persecute me? It hurts you to kick against the goads' (Acts 26:14 RSV). Similarly with the eunuch, Cornelius and Lydia: all were God-fearers of one kind or another and all were searching for truth.

The pattern that emerges, therefore, is one in which the Scriptures, the Spirit and a period of searching all play a part in conversion to Christ. It should be added (although we do not have space to go into this here) that a further general factor was the incorporation of the new converts into the Christian community.

Lessons to be learned

There are four lessons for children's evangelism we should learn from these accounts.

Firstly, *conversion is from beginning to end the work of God.* We can never speak of it as a purely human act. At every stage God is involved even where apparently human processes are at work.

Secondly, *God works through such processes as he himself has ordained.* With the exception of Paul, it was the combination of the Spirit's direct activity within the convert and the God-guided messenger delivering the word through the human process of speech that brought the convert to faith. The function of the evangelist is therefore crucial.

Thirdly, *God spoke to each convert as a person with a personal faith history.* Each one had come to a point where previous beliefs were no longer adequate. Only Christ could give new meaning. In other words, these converts had already gone through a series of faith stages before they were ripe for conversion. This supports rather than rules out the recognition of faith stage development in the process of conversion.

Fourthly, *we must be cautious about applying adult models of conversion of children.* It is significant that nowhere in Acts do we find an account of child conversion. The most we can say is that the accounts point to how God acts towards adults and that by implication he acts similarly towards children. But even here we are speaking theologically: namely that we must reckon that the first three lessons above apply to children as well as adults. What the Acts cases do not do, however, is to provide a technique or a blueprint for converting children as if they were mini-adults.

Conversion or nurture?: children from believing homes

Discussion of conversion brings us back to the question we noted in the previous chapter, namely: how should we view the spiritual status of children from Christian families? Are they to be counted as members of the kingdom until they opt out? Or do they become members only when they consciously opt in by choosing Christ?

Much ink has been expended on this issue, and for good reason: our whole attitude to evangelism among children and families depends upon a clear view of our aim. Put bluntly, are we concerned with conversion or nurture? The theological writer John Inchley made a telling point when he said: 'It is sad to hear Christian parents declaring – "John is saved, though Mary isn't and we are not quite sure about Bill."'[9]

This kind of conversation goes on regularly in Christian households. It is based on the view that no child, even from a believing background, can be counted as a member of God's kingdom until he or she has made an open and conscious declaration of faith. It would seem that the faith of parents counts for nothing.

Such a view has serious implications for the message Christian parents and workers give to children. The aim becomes evangelism rather than nurture. Everything is geared up to conversion. It is assumed that the child of Christian parents needs to 'get saved' in exactly the same way as would a child from an unbelieving home. The pastoral consequences of this can be horrific as the child senses that he can only please his parents by going through some 'conversion' experience which somehow makes him acceptable to them and to God. It is hardly surprising that later years see so many casualties of faith.

> ## It is sad to hear Christian parents declaring – "John is saved, though Mary isn't and we are not quite sure about Bill."

Whilst I am aware that many will subscribe to the belief that children are outside the kingdom until they opt in, I believe, both theologically and pastorally, that children from Christian homes can be affirmed as members of the kingdom until they choose to reject their birthright.

Covenant

To understand this, we have to go back to scripture and the notion of family solidarity. We have seen how the faith of a believing parent (usually the head of the household in biblical times) counted as faith for the family as a whole. Like an umbrella it 'covered' them all. Whether or not individual members held the same belief as the parent, they were all counted by God as members of the covenant relationship established through the parent's faith.[10]

This can be seen in the Old Testament view of covenant. In Genesis 17, we find God entering into a covenant with Abraham. The term covenant means 'promise' or 'agreement'. It was a common means of expressing and sealing a relationship in the Middle East in Old Testament times so that we find covenants between rulers of nations as a way of regulating their affairs.

The covenant between God and Abraham consisted of a twofold promise: that God would pledge himself to Abraham and his descendants and that they would pledge themselves to God. As a result, God would bless them by giving them the Promised Land and his protection. So it was that Israel came to see itself as a covenant people, chosen by God and called to a special relationship with him. 'I will be your God and you will be my people' became the watchword of the nation (Leviticus 26:12).

The basis of the covenant was God's grace. The covenant originated with God and the promise was held out by him. It did not depend upon faith for its *inception* although it had to be *received* by faith. So on the one hand God's promise came to Abraham 'out of the blue' (Genesis 12:2,3) but, on the other, Abraham responded in faith. As Genesis makes clear, 'Abraham believed the Lord, and he credited it to him as righteousness' (Genesis 15:6).

In Old Testament theology, Abraham came to represent Israel. So the nation as a whole was offered the covenant. Moreover, this was not confined to adults who had made an open profession of faith in our modern sense. It applied to all who were born as Israelites. Moreover, it applied to children.

This was emphasised in the rite of circumcision which was not simply a ritual but a sign established and commanded by God to show inclusion within the covenant. God's words to Abraham made this clear: 'You are to undergo circumcision, and it will be the sign of the covenant between me and you' (Genesis 17:11). Genesis 17:12 is explicit that *children* were to receive the sign of covenant acceptance: 'every male who is eight days old must be circumcised, including those born in your household or bought with money from foreigners – those who are not your offspring.'

This is a profound testimony to three theological truths. Firstly, it shows that the *covenant relationship does not depend on faith but upon grace*. Otherwise eight-day-old infants could not have been included. Had acceptance by God depended upon their active individual faith, they would have been excluded from the household of God.

Secondly, it underlines the fact we have already noted: that the *faith of parents covers other members of the household*. This is the significance of the second half of verse 12: even those who are not blood relatives but are nevertheless part of the household are to be circumcised as a sign that they too are included in the covenant. In a home where there is at least one believing parent, it is his or her faith that counts for the rest until they deliberately reject God.

Thirdly, circumcision indicated that *children were to be treated as would-be believers rather than as unbelievers*. The rights and privileges of the covenant relationship were theirs. They participated (as we shall see in Appendix 1) in the full worship life of Israel. There could be no question of their being treated as outsiders: they were counted as insiders until they excluded themselves from God's blessing.

This pattern of relationship (though not the external sign of circumcision) was carried over into the New Testament. As we have seen, the conversion of the Philippian jailer and of Cornelius fits the notion of covenant solidarity.

The implication for us is clear: we must count children of Christians as members of God's kingdom until such time as they refuse God's covenant promise. This means that it becomes more fitting to think of nurture than evangelism for such children. They have to be encouraged to *appropriate and articulate* the blessing they already possess by virtue of their status as covenant children. Once we realise this we free ourselves as parents and evangelists from the enormous pressure to bring about some kind of conversion experience for children who, theologically, are already accepted by God. No less importantly, we also liberate our children from fear, allowing them to become what God has made them: heirs of his covenant promise in Christ.

This, of course, does not directly address the question of children from unbelieving homes (ie the majority in contemporary society). To them, covenant theology would not apply in the same way. However, it is here that we must ask what kind of God it is who established the covenant in the first place. And straight away we are reminded of the

Father of our Lord Jesus Christ, who is both perfectly just and loving – hence the incarnation, the cross and the resurrection. As I have suggested in chapter 6, the biblical picture is of God's justice interpreted by his love; and thus of his grace extending to all children until such time as they reject him. This is not the same as the covenant relationship we have noted above, but it flows from the same God.

Conclusion

We have seen in this chapter that conversion must be thought of both as event *and* as process. These two models offer ways of understanding conversion that are complementary rather than contradictory. What's more, conversion must be studied *both* from the standpoint of faith development theories *and* from the standpoint of Scripture. This is not always an easy match but if we are to be open to insights from both, we must be ready to engage in some tough reasoning. Without such reasoning we run the risk of missing vital truths which can shape our practice of evangelism and our understanding of nurture.

Notes to chapter 7

1 John Westerhoff, *Will Our Children Have Faith?* (revised and expanded edition) Harrisburg, Pa.: Moorehouse Publishing Co., 2000.

2 Westerhoff, as above.

3 Westerhoff, as above.

4 Westerhoff, as above.

5 Though Westerhoff makes it clear that all stages of faith are to be counted within the scope of redemption.

6 Westerhoff, as above.

7 James Fowler, *Stages of Faith,* New York, Harper & Row, 1981, p281.

8 Fowler, as above, pp285–286.

9 John Inchley, *All About Children,* Eastbourne, Coverdale, 1976, p13.

10 For a detailed exposition of covenant theology, see L Berkhof, *Systematic Theology* London, Banner of Truth 1966 edn pp262–304. Also C Brown (ed), *The New International Dictionary of New Testament Theology* vol 1, Exeter, Paternoster 1975, pp365,376. Both show how, despite crucial differences between the old and new covenants, there is an essential continuity.

8 Believing and belonging

Church in crisis

At the start of this book, we saw how dire the situation has become for the churches in Britain as they seek to refashion their ministry to children and young people. In 1989, only 14% of the nation's children had anything to do with church-related Sunday activities. The other 86% were anywhere but in church.[1] That was then. Now the deregulation of Sundays has made the situation even worse. To take but one example: the Church of England alone saw 19,000 fewer under-sixteens attending on Sundays between 1992 and 1994 than before. Research suggests other denominations have fared no better.

The reasons for this are historically and sociologically complex. Certainly, the policies of the churches may not have helped; but by far and away the greatest factor has been the enormous social changes that have taken place over the last half-century. All western societies – even the supposedly religious United States – have become increasingly secularised to the point where the church and the gospel are at the fringes of people's lives at best. Belonging to a congregation is as foreign to most as is the thought of belonging to a sky-diving club. Both are seen as minority hobbies taken up by enthusiasts but not for the majority of ordinary, commonsense folk.

So what has happened to Sundays? The short answer is that they have become merely another leisure day in which church activities compete with everything else. We have only to reflect on the growth of retail shopping to realise this. The opening of huge out-of-town malls as leisure complexes in themselves has meant that shopping has become a typical Sunday leisure activity: sleep in, get up late, eat brunch, spend the majority of the day at the mall, come home, eat an evening meal in front of the TV – this is the pattern for millions of people on the average Sunday. What's more, in a world where adults find themselves more and more stretched during the working week, the use of Sunday as a day to catch up with the regular chores of life or to find precious time for family life has become the norm. In the words of a Church of England report of 1991, '*Responsible parents will regard weekends as quality time for the family and for such good reasons are hardly likely to warm towards local church children's activities on a Sunday.*'[2]

The bottom line is that the churches are reaching no more than a tiny minority of children and young people on the day that is dedicated to God. Those who *are* reached are more or less already part of the church family. For the average (non-churchgoing) family, the thought of going to church doesn't even begin to enter their minds either on Sundays or any other day. Zygmunt Bauman puts it like this:

> ...taxes [must] be paid, dinners cooked, roofs repaired; or
> the brief must be written or studied, letters mailed,
> applications filed, appointments kept, videos repaired,
> tickets bought ... Before one has the time to think of
> eternity, bedtime is coming, and then another day filled to
> the brim with things to be done or undone.[3]

The trend toward decline is not confined to children. When we turn more specifically to teenagers, the picture is no more encouraging. Research published in 1999[4] revealed that in that year:

- The proportion of 15-19 year olds attending church on Sundays continues to decline.
- In England alone, only 6% of this age group worship regularly on Sundays (down from 8% in 1989).
- The 20-29 age group has also dropped by 3% in the same period.
- The total number of churchgoers across the age range has fallen from 5,441,000 in 1979 to 3,714,700 in 1999.

Whichever way we look, the churches are in crisis. However, before we despair absolutely, we need to bear in mind one further social fact: the problem faced by the churches is paralleled by secular youth organisations. Scouts and Guides connected with churches, for example, also dropped by almost 16% for 14-17 year olds and 20% for 18-21 year olds between 1987 and 1993. The habit of joining and sticking with organisations whether religious or secular has been in decline for some years.[5]

Increasing estrangement

When we turn from impersonal statistics to how children and young people actually feel about the church, the picture is no less disturbing. There is an overwhelming sense of estrangement. Responses to surveys include comments such as:

- 'I looked round the church today – why does everyone look so sad? Why can't we have time to get to know each other?'[6]
- 'To make church more interesting for me I would like to watch 5 cartoons on a television hanging on the ceiling.'[7]
- 'What I like about church is when it is finished and it's time to chat to everyone.'[8]

These are comments from children who were habitually attending Sunday worship! When we consider how children perceive matters who hardly, if ever, set foot inside a church, we find ourselves torn between laughter and tears. Here are two sets of comments from youngsters whose lack of experience of church life is typical of the majority. The first is a conversation with an adult who has invited a nine-year old boy, Peter, to a forthcoming service:

> *Peter:* I wouldn't come next week, anyway. I don't like going to church.
> *Adult:* What don't you like about it?
> *Peter:* Well… they sing funny songs.
> *Adult:* Yes, I suppose hymns are a bit funny sometimes! What do you think is funny about them?
> *Peter:* Well, they've got bad language in them.
> *Adult:* (*Pause.*) Bad language?
> *Peter:* Yes. Things like 'God almighty' and 'Jesus Christ'.[9]

This conversation hovers between comedy and tragedy. Peter, brought up in a thoroughly non-churchgoing home, has encountered the names 'God' and 'Jesus' only as swear-words. He knows nothing else about them. And solely on this basis he rejects the idea of attending worship.

Less dramatic – though perhaps more common – is the reaction of two brothers who have been to a church mid-week club but who, despite strong motivation, refuse to follow it up with a visit to church: 'We enjoyed making those Christian Aid posters to go in church for Harvest. But we won't come to the service; our Dad will say we're soft.'[10]

What both conversations bring out is how great a gap exists between the average child and the church. For most purposes, they could be on different planets or inhabit completely different dimensions in time and space. The experience of most children simply doesn't encompass churchgoing except perhaps at Christmas or other special occasions and then usually with Mums, Grandmas and sisters rather than with Dads and Granddads. Or to put it differently, the church – and along with it, the Christian faith – is largely irrelevant as far as most children's real-life worlds are concerned.

This is a drastic conclusion but the evidence supports it. The notion of belonging to a regular worshipping Christian community is as distant from the thoughts of most children as Earth is from the Milky Way.

But if *belonging* is a non-starter, what about *believing*?

Increasing scepticism

Here the evidence is harder to interpret. The 1994 Teenage Religion and Values Survey found that by the age of thirteen, 39% of young people said they believed in God, 26% said they didn't, while 35% were uncertain.[11] When we turn to younger age groups, there is little reliable data.

However, the educationalist David Hay has suggested that whereas even only a few years ago the usual age at which young people overtly began to disown religious belief was typically twelve or thirteen (the onset of puberty in which they were also seriously confronted with scientific reasoning for the first time), this has now dropped to as young as nine or ten. Scepticism is being shown at an ever-earlier age. Speaking of western societies, he notes that: 'It is around the age of 12 that children ... typically have their first serious induction into the scientific tradition of the Enlightenment, with its associated religious scepticism. That children are now often receiving instruction from a much younger age may have the effect of inhibiting early spirituality at an even more sensitive, vulnerable stage.'[12]

What are we to make of this? Superficially, it's tempting to conclude that children simply cease to believe in God at a younger and younger age. But surely this is too simple. Can belief evaporate just like that?

Buried belief

David Hay thinks not. In his view, children don't stop believing; but they do find it increasingly difficult to express belief once they enter a stage where to do so is regarded as unacceptable, sissy or unscientific. In other words, when they feel their peer group, or significant adults around them (eg parents or teachers) prefer them to avoid religion altogether. Remember the words of the brothers quoted above: 'Dad will say we're soft.' They could just as easily have said, with their peers in mind: 'It's not cool.'

The notion of belonging to a regular worshipping Christian community is as distant from the thoughts of most children as Earth is from the Milky Way.

How has such a situation arisen? To be sure, the general process of secularisation we noted in chapter one has played a large part. But, specifically, for nearly 300 years, western culture has systematically made it more and more difficult to express any kind of beliefs in other than scientific or quasi-scientific language. To gain 'street cred', it becomes necessary to use the language of science (or at least appear to do so). Anything else will either be regarded as inferior or disregarded altogther. Reference to religion or the spiritual will automatically be thought of as cranky or misguided. At best it will be seen as a purely personal matter. Thus, 'The adult world into which our children are inducted is more often than not destructive to their spirituality.'[13]

What has been shut out by the front door, however, has a habit of sneaking in by the back. The researches conducted by Hay and others into the spiritual lives of children demonstrate that the process described above has not destroyed belief – it has merely suppressed it. When questioned sensitively and appropriately, children from all backgrounds and in various settings speak freely of their awareness of God or spiritual experience. The publication by Hay and Rebecca Nye of their careful research into children's attitudes is full of conversations with children which illustrate this. One in particular stands out: John, a six year old, attended church only twice a year yet had firm Christian beliefs. Asked how he came to hold them, he replied,

> I worked about it and I received… one day… I was with
> my mum and I begged her… um… for me to go to um…
> some church. And we did it and… I prayed… and after that
> praying… I knew that good was on my side. And I heard
> him in my mind say this: 'I am with you. Every step you
> go. The Lord is with you. May sins be forgiven.'[14]

What John experienced seems on any reckoning to have been an encounter with God. True, it may not have been a standard evangelical conversion but nonetheless for a six year old, the story he recounts is amazing. Even more astonishing – given his lack of church background – is the next bit:

> Well once I went um… in the night and I saw this bishopy
> kind of alien. I said, 'Who are you?' And he said, 'I am the
> Holy Spirit.' I did think he was the Holy Spirit.[15]

John's mother subsequently told him he could not have spoken to the Holy Spirit since the latter looks like a ball of fire (she was not a church-goer but had some residual Bible imagery in mind). Nonetheless, John still commented that afterwards 'I often felt the Holy Spirit in me.'

At one level, it's difficult to know exactly what did happen. Did John undergo a genuine religious experience of God's Spirit or not, and what does John's story tell us about the openness and capacity of children towards God? Also, what does John's story tell us about the reality of God's grace being already present and active ahead of any human inter-vention?

John, though, was six – well below the age at which Hay argues that a scientific worldview begins to suppress openness towards religious ideas. What about older children?

Here we find evidence both of a willingness to describe spiritual expe-riences but also of a growing struggle. Ten year old Jenny, for example, could speak of the time 'that I stop and think, "How did I get here?" Well, that's when I switch onto God. That's when I start thinking about him.'[16] Yet asked why she had found a particular hymn meaningful, she found it difficult to talk freely in religious language: 'You think it's quite easy [when singing it], but when you try to explain it ... you don't know which words to use.'[17] Rebecca Nye goes on to describe her research conversations with Jenny's contemporaries as follows:

> For others it was apparent that embarrassment was at the
> root of their reluctance. They were cautious of straying for
> too long beyond the acceptable confines of secular
> discourse. Some children admitted they were afraid of
> being laughed at or thought stupid or even mad ... if they
> talked about their personal sense of the religious in their
> lives.[18]

What all this points to is a highly complex situation. On one hand, we have the vast majority of children estranged from the church. Yet on the other, there is clear evidence of an underlying capacity for spiritual awareness and even commitment despite the pressures of peers and adults to suppress or ridicule them. This poses a unique challenge for children's evangelism. It is to the strategies required by such a challenge we now turn.

A new approach

In its most simplistic form, the conventional logic of evangelism – whether directed towards adults or children – has run something like this: first, find your audience (usually through some kind of special event); second, preach the gospel; third, invite commitment; fourth, encourage those who have indicated commitment to join a church and become disciples. This is what might be termed the *believe and belong* model: belonging to a community of faith is the outcome of believing in Christ. First believe, then belong.

This is the approach in which I (and many like me) was schooled. It was adopted by children's workers for decades from the earliest beach and caravan missions to today's modern approaches. Where would we be without it?

But, given the complex situation described in the first half of this chapter, I want to suggest that rather than abandoning or abolishing it we also need to look at the alternative strategies which exist.

If the traditional model was based on believe-then-belong, the alternative approach could be thought of as belong-then-believe.

Put simply, the belong-then-believe approach starts from the view that individuals, whether they are five, fifteen or fifty years old, are not isolated beings who come to faith in Christ by a process of hearing the gospel and thinking individualistically about it. Rather, they are already social beings who come to the gospel with a cluster of views, beliefs and feelings pre-formed by their participation in family, community, society and culture. This is the point we have noted in chapter one. In other words, individual *belief* cannot be separated from social *belonging*.

Now in the traditional evangelism model, this is recognised but only *after* the individual has come to personal faith in Christ. What it says, in effect, is something like this: 'Believe as an individual then you can belong to the group': believe-belong.

But turn things around. We invite children (or adults for that matter) to belong to the group first, then to believe: belong-believe. They become members of the faith-seeking group first, then they discover the reality of Jesus for themselves by virtue of being part of that group. Belonging to the group precedes personal faith, not the other way round as the conventional approach assumes. Individuals do not come to Christ first as a precondition of becoming members of the faith-group: they are members prior to discovering Christ.

This may seem like hair-splitting but the implications are considerable. Consider the diagram on the opposite page.

In the first drawing, the hard circle represents the fixed boundary of belief that defines whether or not someone is a member of the community of faith. They can belong inside the circle only by believing certain things such as that Jesus is the Son of God and that he has died for our sins. (Different faith groups would draw up different lists of what constitutes an adequate set of beliefs to qualify for getting inside the circle.) The crucial thing is that there is a clearly defined boundary that decides whether an individual is in or out. Once inside, they belong to the faith-community which undertakes to nurture them. In this diagram, *belonging is the outcome of believing*.

In the second drawing, there is no hard and fast boundary. Instead, the focus is the centre which represents the centrality of Jesus to Christian faith and life. The key issue, then, is not whether individuals have

 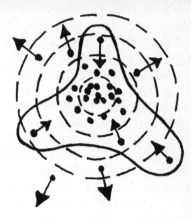

Model A: believe – belong   Model B: belong – believe[19]

crossed a boundary defined by certain beliefs but *in which direction they are moving*. Are they looking towards Christ or not? Are they moving towards him or away from him? Do they belong to those whose line-of-sight is towards Jesus or do they belong to those whose line-of-sight points elsewhere? On this model, it is direction not boundary that is important. Belonging is defined by whether someone is moving towards the centre which is Christ rather than by whether they believe certain doctrinal propositions. As Monica Hill puts it, 'The concern is not with uniformity but with movement towards the centre. Some are far away, coming from another direction. Nearness is the dimension of biblical knowledge, spiritual growth and commitment to Jesus Christ who is the Centre.'[20]

It is important to realise in this second model, however, that beliefs are not irrelevant. Knowing and following Jesus is a matter of believing certain truths as well as emotional gravitation. As we have seen in our earlier discussion of faith, the believing component is essential; for how could we know we were moving towards the centre unless we had some idea of who Jesus is and what he has done?

Hill makes this clear. But unlike the first model, belonging to the faith-group does not first require crossing a fixed boundary. It requires us to be looking in the same direction as fellow believer-seekers and moving with them. Believing does not *precede* belonging but is part and parcel of the same directional movement. Indeed, it may be the fact of belonging to the faith-group that produces and reinforces belief so that belonging leads to believing.

We can perhaps illustrate the difference between the two models by imagining two churches. The first, West Hill Independent Church decides to hold a series of five evangelistic evenings for children and invites an outside evangelist to speak at them. The programme is designed to preach the gospel and to challenge those who attend to give their lives to Christ. Each evening concludes with a Bible message and invitation for the children to come to Jesus with the help of counsellors. Once they have done so, they will be invited to attend Sunday activities so as to help them grow in their new-found faith. The aim is clear: believe so that you may belong. You cannot be inside the circle of faith until you have consciously believed in Christ. Once this has happened, you're in.

The second church, Trinity Community Church, has a different approach. It too wants to share the gospel with children but has decided to organise a series of kids club evenings every Wednesday for six weeks. Along with lots of fun activities, each evening will contain Bible-based teaching aimed at encouraging children to understand more about Christ. Only at the end of six weeks will an evangelistic invitation be issued. In the meantime, attenders will be invited to join Sunday activities if they wish but this is not a requirement. The organisers make it clear that attendance on Wednesdays is their primary aim.

What's the difference between the approaches adopted by the two churches? At first, it may seem very little: simply the postponement of an evangelistic invitation till the end of the sixth evening.

In fact, the difference is far greater than that. It is a matter of two distinct views of the relationship between believing and belonging. At West Hill, the view is that a short, sharp mission will bring children to a point of decision quickly so that they can then join the church. Not until they have made a commitment can they be counted as belonging.

Trinity views the matter differently. They have deliberately delayed any evangelistic invitation until the children have had time to form relationships in the context of weekly activities designed not to pressurise them but to enable them to build a sense of belonging. During this period, they will be introduced to teaching about Jesus in such a way that he is presented as a character they want to know more about. The picture they will build up over six weeks will give them a chance to make up their own minds as to whether they want to move in his direction or not. Moreover, the invitation (when it comes) will be as much to continue as members of the Kids Club who enjoy weekly activities together as it will be to come to individually-professed faith in him. The two are seen as going hand in hand. The organisers reckon that professions of faith in Christ will happen in due course as children make up their minds about which direction they want to travel. Being individuals, of course, they will do so at their own pace, though they will always be with fellow-travellers who are heading in the same direction.

In these two examples, as the reader will already have guessed, West Hill represents the 'fixed boundary' approach to evangelism. Belonging is defined by believing: evangelism is designed to produce belief first and belonging second. By contrast, Trinity embodies the 'directional' approach. Believing is encouraged by belonging. Being a member of the faith-group is the way into belief rather than the outcome of it.

There is a place for both approaches provided that they are seen as complementary rather than rivals and provided that each is suited to its context. However, it may be that in today's world, the majority of unchurched children will best be reached by an approach which aims first and foremost at developing a sense of group belonging before it invites individual commitment to Christ. My own view is that this fits well with the processes of faith development I have outlined in earlier chapters.

So what about traditional beach missions and holiday weeks? These are necessarily compressed into a few days which alters the dynamic and 'feel' of activities, particularly if they take place in a residential setting. Historically, many operated on the traditional believe-belong model and experience shows that many children came to faith in Christ in this way over the years. However, increasingly the belong-believe model can make great use of the strong sense of community (albeit temporary) created by mission and holiday weeks, which can be a great backdrop to sharing faith.

But what about the objection that it is impossible to belong to the community of faith without first having demonstrated belief? To this, I find myself replying that if the insights of faith development theory are in any way true or if the theological argument I have put forward in the previous chapters has any validity, children should be counted inside the kingdom of God until they explicitly renounce it. Moreover, if the model of belonging and believing is allowed, the need to show adherence to a set of beliefs before being counted inside the circle of faith is removed. Belonging is a matter of being with others on the same faith journey rather than being judged by profession of certain articles of faith.

Given the situation described earlier by David Hay and Rebecca Nye, children who are discouraged from talking about spiritual experiences or issues at home or school or among their peers may need a long period of time in which to build up relationships and confidence. Only when they see it is okay to speak about such experiences and questions will they be able to open their hearts deeply in such a way as to discover the love of Christ for themselves. They need to belong before they can believe, or express belief. In short, belonging first, believing second.

Conclusions

What kind of evangelistic strategies might be appropriate in the light of all I have said? It is important to grasp that I am not arguing for one model alone. Churches must think carefully about which will best fit the needs of those it is seeking to reach. It will be important to choose an approach that fits the immediate context and people rather than one that happens to suit the predilections or experience of the church's leaders.

But whichever approach is chosen, the need to create a sense of belonging will be paramount. This is as true of the conventional mission as of the mid-week club. Only when they feel able to engage with spiritual questions without being ridiculed or sidelined will children from non-Christian homes open themselves to the gospel in all its fullness. Whether this is in the context of a five-day evangelistic campaign or whether in a longer-term environment, the point remains the same: belonging will facilitate believing. This is the radical message we need to hear and practise.

Notes to chapter 8

1   For details see the Church of England report *All God's Children?* London, National Society/Church House Publishing 1991, p3.

2   Above, p22.

3   Zygmunt Bauman, *Postmodernity and Its Discontents,* Cambridge, Polity Press 1997, p169.

4   Peter Brierley (ed), *The Tide is Running Out,* Bromley, Christian Research 2000.

5   *Youth a Part: Young People and the Church*, London, National Society/Church House Publishing, 1996, p13.

6   General Synod Board of Education, *Children in the Way,* London, National Society/Church House Publishing, 1988, p 26. Extracts are copyright © The National Society and are reproduced by permission.

7   *Children in the Way,* p8.

8   *Children in the Way,* p26.

9   *Children in the Way,* p18.

10   *Children in the Way,* p19.

11   Leslie J. Francis, William K. Kay, Alan Kerby and Olaf Fogwill, *Fast-moving Currents in Youth Culture,* Oxford/Sutherland, Lynx 1995, p166.

12   David Hay with Rebecca Nye, *The Spirit of the Child,* London: HarperCollins 1998, p50.

13   Hay/Nye, p21.

14   Hay/Nye, p102.

15   Hay/Nye, p102.

16   Hay/Nye, p106.

17   Hay/Nye, p105.

18   Hay/Nye, p105.

19   Illustration from *Youth A Part*, as above, p14. Illustration copyright © Central Board of Finance, 1996, and is reproduced by permission.

20   Quoted in *Youth a Part,* as above, p15.

Appendix 1: Children, worship and Communion

W hat are the most important questions surrounding children and worship? In my view, they're not the commonly-asked 'how to' questions: how to lead worship, organise a service, choose appropriate material and so on. Although crucial, these are second-order issues[1] that flow from more fundamental questions. It is these first-order questions which are the most important; and we shall be considering them in this chapter. They revolve around three issues:

- Power: who holds it, how is it used and where do children fit in?
- Inclusiveness: how are children and young people included in the worship life of a church?
- Theology: what justifies different approaches to children and worship? How are we to decide?

This chapter, therefore, will focus not on the practicalities of leading all-age worship but on the principles that should govern it. And because, in New Testament terms, the Lord's Supper (or Holy Communion) is the central act of worship for Christians – it is, after all, the only such act commanded by Jesus (Luke 22:17–20) – the issue of children and Communion will be discussed at some length. How the Church treats its children around the Lord's table is perhaps indicative of how it regards the place of children in worship generally.

But these are big issues. One way to think about them would be to work through them essay-style, much as other chapters in part two of this book have been written. However, in what follows we shall adopt a different course.

Imagine you are invited to eavesdrop on a conference on the subject of children, young people and worship. A number of speakers have been asked to present papers on various aspects and to answer questions. What might the transcript of such a conference look like? In what follows, you're invited to use your imagination. The papers are fictional and not exhaustive; but they do open up the issues. And for those interested in reading more, the endnotes offer suggestions.

Session 1: Setting the scene

A large hall is filled with people. Most are in their thirties and forties. A few are older. In the back row a small group of teenagers also sits. On the platform a semi-circle of men and women is seated. The woman in the centre rises to address the hall:

Chair: Welcome to this conference on children, young people and worship. Our theme is very dear to many people's hearts: how far the modern church takes its children and young people seriously in the very activity that gives it life - worship. This is a large subject and to help us I am glad to welcome on your behalf a distinguished panel of speakers who will, in turn, address the conference. Later there will be opportunity for questions from the floor. This afternoon, we shall be working in seminar groups on different topics.

I turn now to our first pair of speakers: Mrs Jeanne Livingstone from St Timothy's Church and her colleague Mr Ben Stanley. Jeanne and Ben, we look forward to your presentation. (*Applause.*)

Jeanne: Thank you. I am not here today as an academic expert but simply as a mother of three. My children – Lucy, Fiona and Adam – range from ages seventeen to ten, in that order. We have been members of St Tim's since Lucy was born. My husband Jack and I have done our best to raise our children in the Christian faith. But this hasn't always been easy. Not only have we encountered the usual difficulties that every parent faces; but we have also found it hard to worship as a family within the church. It's about this I want to talk this morning.

When Lucy was born, we had her baptised. That was a good experience because it gave us an opportunity to rediscover our own spiritual roots (which had got a little dry over the years). The preparation classes were excellent and the service well done. It set the seal upon us as a Christian family and made Lucy feel welcome within the family of the church. When Fiona and Adam came along, we did the same for them.

During the years that followed, St Tim's provided all kinds of activities for kids. On Sundays, while Jack and I were in church, there was a large, well-staffed Sunday school. All we had to do was to drop the kids off as we went into worship and collect them afterwards. On Wednesday evenings, the church ran an after-school club which was a real hit with churched and unchurched children alike. Add in the summer camps and the Christmas parties and you have a picture of a thriving children's work.

It wasn't until Lucy reached her teens we began to realise that this system, that had served her so well, had a downside to it. The great strength throughout the years had been the development of peer group solidarity. Church kids would hang out together, do things together and were generally inseparable. You can imagine what a relief it was for us parents to know this.

The problem was that this peer group mentality had been built up independently of the worship life of the adults in the church. The Sunday school system split off the kids from the grown-ups. Our church was in effect two churches. And once Lucy's group became too old for Sunday school, they had no place to go for worship. They tried the adult services a few times but found them boring and irrelevant. (Kids can be pretty judgmental, can't they?)

Because they hadn't been encouraged to attend worship except on special occasions, worshipping with adults was totally unfamiliar. The liturgy, the music, the sermons were all geared to their parents. For them it was like living on another planet.

Needless to say, the group gradually stopped coming to church. They continued to meet as a youth group but worshipping with the rest of the church was out. They still look back fondly to their Sunday school days but have never made the transition to adult worship and involvement in the life of St Tim's.

Belatedly, the church has set about trying to reconstruct its children's work. Sunday school (now renamed) still exists; but they begin each Sunday by coming into worship with adults for ten minutes before going off to their own activities. There is also a regular all-age service too, so some progress has been made.

But, by and large, the attitude of adults is that the young people should join in worship on adult terms. "After all," the attitude runs, "they have been given a solid Christian grounding in Sunday school; so why shouldn't they take their place as young adults in adult worship?" A few far-sighted people see that this won't work, but the majority expect the youngsters to come in on adult terms. They don't seem to appreciate that just because we have a strong Sunday school, this doesn't guarantee a strong teenage work. Jack has recently been elected to the Church Council and hopes to challenge the entrenched attitude of some of those in positions of leadership. But that will take time which we don't have. I feel sorry for the vicar who is caught in the middle.

So, my hope for this conference is that I shall go back with some positive ideas to get debate going at St Tim's. I also hope that sharing my own experience will encourage others in the same position to see they're not alone. Thank you. (*Applause*)

Chair: We're grateful to you, Jeanne, for your candour. Many of us will identify with the situation you have described. In a few minutes we'll come back to you for questions. But before we do so, let me call upon Ben Stanley, an adviser on children's and youth work for the diocese in which Jeanne lives, to offer some further insights and reflections upon the questions she has raised. (*Applause.*)

Ben: Let me begin by assuring Jeanne that her story is not uncommon. In my work I see many similar situations, some of which have recovered, some of which have not. It sounds as if the jury is still out on how children's and young people's work will develop at St Tim's.

What's the central issue at stake in Jeanne's story and in all our discussions about children and worship? Is it what you do on Sundays? Is it how to motivate young people to move on from a Sunday school way of life? Is it to do with encouraging children to switch from passive dependency to active responsibility?

I want to suggest that important though these questions are, the core issue has to do with the exercise of power. It underlies all of them. Now I won't be popular in some quarters for saying this: power remains something of a dirty word among Christians. But in my twenty years of working with churches, I have become more and more convinced that power is the key.

What do I mean?

Jeanne has described a church that has a thriving children's work. But once the children graduate from Sunday school they run into massive institutional blockages as far as Sunday worship is concerned. Why is this so?

Put simply, the adults hold all the power and call all the shots. After all, when we stop to reflect how Sunday school has been run, I'll bet it's been a matter of the adults deciding when and where it should meet, what it should teach, how it should be organised and so on. Although ostensibly a children's group, it has been an organisation run by adults, along adult lines, according to what adults think is needed and, unfortunately sometimes, to meet the needs of adults (namely, childminding while they get on with worship).

Happily this arrangement has worked as long as the desires of the kids and the adults have coincided for the first ten or eleven years of the children's lives. This, after all, is the period when children are dependent on adults and expect to follow what adults tell them.

Everything, therefore, is geared to a system in which children have no power and very little say in how things are run. This is OK for the junior school years but once children reach adolescence, the independence hormone kicks in and everything becomes a power struggle.

In the home setting, the struggle is worked through – albeit painfully – as both youngsters and adults learn to make adjustments, concessions and agreements. But in institutions, the process is much harder. It requires a considerable degree of sensitivity on the part of those who run the institution to recognise the need for accommodations and to make them. Churches do not have a good track record on this.

The crunch comes when the young people know they are too old for Sunday school but have only the adult services to go to. How do they enter into the bargaining process they would engage in if it were a matter of domestic life? Unless the church has leaders and structures that allow power to be shared across the adult/young people divide, negotiation simply can't take place. Adults hold fast to their own bit of territory while youngsters are presented with a stark choice: either you come in on our (adult) terms or you do your own thing.

Nine times out of ten, this kind of ultimatum is met by withdrawal. All is not lost if this means withdrawing into the youth group or youth service; for while they're still connected with church in some way, there's at least hope. But where withdrawal means pulling away from church altogether, it's a failure of the first order. What's worse, adults often blame the teenagers for being immature or, alternatively, put it down to a combination of the age we live in and the rebelliousness of youth.

The irony is, of course, that these selfsame adults will lament the loss of young people but will at the same time refuse to make any changes that would allow them to play a fuller part in the life of the church. It's a classic double-bind in which everyone loses.

In my view, then, power is the issue. Until those who control it – that is, adults – recognise that they must yield it, they will merely perpetuate the status quo. This, as we have seen, is likely to leave more and more congregations without an entire generation of members. Is this a future we can afford?

Chair: Ben, we have appreciated your thought-provoking argument. There will be many here who have probably never thought about children in power terms. Yet you have forced us to do so, even if that makes us uneasy. We now have the opportunity to give you and Jeanne some feedback through questions. I hope you both feel free to continue to speak your minds. Let me start by inviting questions specifically to Jeanne.

Questioner: Jeanne, you began by referring to yourself not as an expert but as a parent. What skills, gifts and insights do you think parents bring to the debate over children and worship?

Jeanne: On one level, there are basic instinctual insights parents bring which can be useful in designing, planning and even leading worship that's appropriate for both children and adults. After all, we're the ones who are with our children much more than worship leaders or Sunday school teachers. We see what interests our kids, what motivates them, how they respond and so on.

So I would say there's room for parents in, say, a worship planning team where they can contribute positively to discussion about what will work and what won't. They can also act as a conduit between leaders and children so that ideas that crop up in the planning group can be tried out in advance on children at home and feedback brought to the group. The alternative is for an all-adult group to make the decisions solely on the basis of what *they* think is best.

Questioner: Would you include young people in such a group?

Jeanne: Most definitely.

Ben: If I can jump in for a moment, I'd like to support what Jeanne has just said. To include young people in planning, designing and executing worship sends a very strong message about the leadership's attitude to power. For a start it signals that power is there to be shared rather than hoarded. It also tells the whole church – not least the young people – that worship is not the preserve of a few adults but is the work of the whole people of God, whatever their age. On a purely pragmatic level, it is likely to staunch the outflow of youngsters because it makes them feel they have some ownership. They feel valued and wanted.

Questioner: Does that mean you would include children of any age for the purposes of planning or leading worship?

Jeanne: I can't speak for Ben but I would be quite careful about choosing the kids to be involved and about allocating tasks to them that were appropriate. Different ages will be able to cope with different tasks. Take planning, for instance. I know of a church which has a planning group for their monthly all-age worship consisting of the minister, the music group leader, two parents from different homes, two ten-year-old girls and a fourteen-year-old boy. It works quite well: the group decides what will go into services; and if they need expertise not contained in the group, they ask somebody to join them who has it.

Likewise with the leading of worship. The same church has small teams of people – mainly laity – that include children and teenagers who assist in the leading of services. And of course in addition to standing up front, there are lots of ways in which kids and adults can work together to make the practicalities of a service happen – giving out books to worshippers as they arrive and taking up the offering are just two examples. There are plenty of possibilities if you are minded to look for them.

Ben: Though Jeanne is right, we need to remember that what we're talking about is not adults sharing power at the margins but at the *centre* of the church's life. This means a change in the mindset both of leaders and of the whole congregation so that kids are thought of as 'us' rather than 'them'. It also means the youngsters themselves learning to be less dependent and more like partners.

Questioner: I find myself warming to what Jeanne has said but I have to say to Ben that I think his views on power are somewhat ideological and even cynical. Is he saying that church leaders are power-mad or that all adults are simply on some kind of power trip? Surely this demeans everyone and denies that God is at work?

Ben: Hmm, I can see I've stirred up some strong feelings. Please don't hear me as suggesting that the church is just about power. I'm not. But the reason I've stressed the issue of power is that it's so rarely considered. We're much more comfortable analysing our congregations in spiritual terms.

But the truth is that in any group of people, whether it's the church or the local tennis club, power relationships will inevitably and necessarily develop. Somebody has to exercise leadership and make decisions on behalf of the whole group, which means that power has to come into play. After all, one definition of power is the ability to get things done. And since we all want things done, the use of power is inevitable.

So what's the key issue? It's how power is arrived at, distributed and exercised. And that's where we come back to the need for congregations and their leaders to be ruthlessly self-aware and self-critical. They need to ask who holds power, how they got it, how they're using it and, most of all, who benefits. Even asking these basic questions can be immensely fruitful provided that people are genuinely open to hearing God tell them they need to change and being willing to do it.

Questioner: That's all very well in theory but how would it apply in real life, especially in the area of children and worship?

Ben: Let me suggest a number of ways. Jeanne has already spoken about the planning and leading of worship, so I will focus on the wider questions of how children are included in the structures of the church.

Suppose we begin with my earlier questions: Who's in control? Who holds the power? Answers might include: the minister, the eldership, the diaconate, the church council, the congregation, or even an outside body such as the diocese or regional council. Now ask yourself how they got there. Was it by appointment, by election, by convention, tradition or what? If it's by election, of course, the process has a certain openness and fairness about it. And the wider the electorate, the more open the election, the fairer and more representative will be the result.

Take, for example, the church council. Who's allowed to vote for it? Probably all the church members. But what about the children? Are they entitled to vote? Are they entitled to stand for election? Probably not, at least until they're seventeen or so – in which case they're hardly kids any more.

But why aren't children allowed to have a say in who represents them and who makes their views known? The answer (although adults might not want to admit it) is that they are presumed not to be capable either of holding office or of making a sensible judgment about who to vote for.

Now pause for a moment and think about the implications of what's being said. To exclude youngsters from the decision-making structures is effectively to deny they are full members of the Body of Christ. Is this really what we believe? Surely, in any theology of the church, children and young people are members of the Body as much as are adults. And to exclude them from a say in how the Body is run on the grounds of a purely arbitrary age limit is neither just nor loving: it is simply power politics.

Questioner: So you think children of any age ought to be included in all the structures of church life? That would be chaotic. They would be voting for things they didn't understand and were probably bored with anyway.

Ben: With all due respect, that's exactly the kind of attitude which has created the problems of exclusion we're talking about today. I'm not advocating that there should be no age limit or other criteria for admitting children as candidates for office or as electors. That would be absurd. At some point there has to be a trade-off between the principle of competence and the principle of representation. A three-year-old would find it hard to act as a representative. But for some purposes, a ten-year-old could – and a twelve-year-old certainly.

If you doubt this, just think about how schools are run. My daughter has been an elected member of her school council since she was eleven (she's now seventeen). All the members are elected by their peers who, by and large, seem well able to choose representatives who can competently represent them and do the business of the council. They make decisions about the running of the school, have a budget and elect their members each year – just like most church councils in fact.

Now it's true they have only a limited area of decision-making. The school's board of governors decides the strategic policy issues and allocates the really big money. But at its own level, the school council works. And if it can work in secular education, why can't a version of it work in the church?

One way would be to set aside, say, three places on the church council for youngsters between the ages of eleven and sixteen. Young people between those ages would be eligible to stand for office and to vote for candidates in that age band. They wouldn't be able to vote for adults; and adults wouldn't be allowed to vote for them. In effect, it would be an electoral college specifically designed for those who have no other way of entering the decision-making structures even though they are profoundly affected by them. There are, no doubt, other approaches that could be tried. In a sense, it doesn't matter which one you opt for as long as it achieves the objective of including young people on a fair and equitable basis.

Chair: (*intervening*) I'm afraid, Ben, our time has run out. I don't want to cut you off prematurely, but before we close this first part of our conference, I would like to give Jeanne a chance to have the last word.

Jeanne: Thank you, Chair. There's not a lot I would wish to add to what both of us have already said. I'm conscious that we've offered a lot of thoughts in a short space of time and that this may leave some people feeling a bit overwhelmed. I do want, however, to underline two things. Firstly, that while I haven't spoken in the same way as Ben about power, I believe him to be absolutely right. Although I might quibble with one or two points in his analysis, broadly speaking I think he's correct: we can't run away from power issues when dealing with the place of children in the church and we would be wrong to do so. Secondly, the time is running short. Already, more than 50% of churches in our diocese have fewer than ten teenagers and many of them have none at all. We owe it to the swathes of young people growing up inside and outside our churches to find ways of making them feel welcome rather than abandoning them to the world.

(*The conference then broke up for coffee.*)

Session 2: The discussion continues

People return to the hall after their break. There is a lively buzz as the Chair calls for order.

Chair: I hope you have all enjoyed your coffee. Following two provocative and stimulating papers from Jeanne Livingstone and Ben Stanley, we shall now move on to a paper by Dr Helen Michaels who is a nationally-known specialist on how faith grows in children and families. Helen, welcome: we look forward to your paper on the implications of faith development for worship.

Helen: Thank you for inviting me to this very important occasion. The subject of children and the church has been creeping up the church's agenda for about three decades. In the last ten years, this has sharpened into the issue of children and worship. Only now are we beginning to take children seriously not (as the cliché goes) as the church of the future but as the church of the present. I hope in the next few minutes to outline some of the more recent thinking that has appeared under the heading of faith development studies.

To many people, the idea of 'faith development' will be new. We're all accustomed to the thought that faith grows as we mature in Christ, but the notion of 'faith development studies' is something that has arrived on the church's horizon only in the past few years. Even now, it is unfamiliar to most of us. But I predict it will become increasingly important as a tool for thinking about mission, pastoral care, discipleship – in fact the whole of Christian life.

Where it becomes important for children and worship is in its explanation of how children develop in their spiritual lives. Worship, of course, is central to this and therefore faith development and worship are closely related.

The core idea is that children go through a series of stages from birth onwards, in which faith grows and develops with clear characteristics that can be ascribed to each stage. You have already received a briefing document outlining James Fowler's theories in your conference pack, so I shall touch only on the main points as they are relevant.

The first point we need to notice is that we all have faith of some kind from an early age. This may not be Christian faith or indeed religious faith at all. It may be faith in a secular belief, a person, a way of life or a worldview. But it's faith nonetheless. This is very important: we are faith-beings. But in terms of specifically religious faith, it follows that there will be *appropriate forms of worship relative to each faith stage*. These forms will express the characteristics found in any given stage. Worship that is appropriate for pre-school stages, for example, will not be identical to that which is fitting for junior school children or teenagers.

Now we all know this intuitively and may regard what I have just said as a matter of common sense. But what faith development studies enable us to do is to think about the subject with a lot of evidence from education, psychology and theology to enable us to construct acts of worship that reflect *a range of faith stages* rather than only one, or the lowest common denominator between stages.

So, what would an all-stage (as opposed to an all-age) service look like? And how would we set about preparing it?

For a start, we would ask ourselves what characteristics are distinctive to different stages and which ones are common to all stages. Once we have decided what the distinctives are, we can select activities that appropriately express them.

For the early faith stages, we might reckon that lots of play and affirmatory adult attention was the key. Children in these stages (probably up to five years old) would be in worship for only brief periods of time. They would need something expressly geared to them: an invitation to come to the front and play on the floor, perhaps, while everyone else got on with the service. Or a simple story and song. They could then be escorted to another part of the room or the church to do playgroup-type things.

For the next stages, the use of more complex story and song is appropriate, possibly backed up with some sort of practical activity. Since children enjoy finding out things and asking and answering questions at this stage, an activity that involves questions and discovery might work well. This could take the form of a quiz that the whole congregation might join in; or it could be something the children engage in while adults are doing their own thing. The point is that it doesn't have to be too didactic. And it doesn't mean that children have to spend the whole time away from adults. I once visited a church in Northern Ireland where all ages joined together for a time of praise and testimony for about fifteen minutes at the start of the service. In this the children, as well as the adults, were encouraged to choose songs and speak. There then followed a discovery session for the kids in the next room while the adults got on with learning together. In their discovery session, the youngsters had practical activities that stretched their reading and craft skills without seeing these simply as a reinforcement to a traditional Sunday school-type lesson. The activities genuinely were child-centred in which they worked in pairs or groups to achieve clearly-defined tasks. After they had finished (by which time the adults had heard a Bible reading and sermon) the kids rejoined everyone else and shared something of what they had done.

Now this might sound a bit too good to be true. In terms of preparation, it was certainly very time-intensive. The key, however, was (a) a clear understanding, on the part of the leaders, of what was appropriate to the different stages represented among the children; and (b) active encouragement from the congregation as a whole for this approach. What's more, the adults didn't operate with a hidden assumption that what was going on with the children was somehow inferior to what the adults were doing. There was a wide understanding that everyone, no matter what age or stage, was on a journey of faith together and that all stages were equally valid. This was terribly important.

Could this work in every situation? I don't know. But what does seem clear is that when there is an understanding of what faith development theory has to offer, accompanied by a commitment to take risks in testing it out, such an approach can pay enormous dividends.

So much for making connections between the distinctive characteristics of each stage and components of worship. Does this mean it's difficult for a cross-section of stages to worship together?

Here we must come back to those characteristics that span the stages. What are they? I suggest a few: (1) the importance of story – which theologians have come to recognise plays a central role for adult theological reflection and is not simply a childish device; (2) the use of imagination

– this cuts across all ages and stages; (3) the dramatic character of worship, especially where simple liturgy is used that adds an element of structure akin to the theatre. (After all, who doesn't like theatre, whatever their age?); (4) the sense of fun and play – why do you think adults enjoy the high jinks that go on in family services and are willing to accept things that they would frown upon in other kinds of worship? (5) the use of symbol – one of the most powerful all-stage and all-age services I go to regularly is the annual Christingle service. It is full of symbolism central to the Christian gospel, light versus darkness being the most obvious, and the church is always packed not just with regular worshippers but with those who come only once or twice a year. Good use of symbol can evoke a deep chord across the stages.

This is not an exhaustive list, but it does get us thinking. All these features are present to some degree from the earliest stages, once we get past the baby stage. In some stages one feature may be more developed than in others, but they are all there to an extent. The trick is to use faith development insights to apply them differentially according to the balance of stages in the congregation. I could elaborate for some considerable time; but on that note, Chair, I think I had better draw to a close.'

Chair: We have greatly appreciated your expertise and practical knowledge, Helen. As we are running short of time, I hope you will be ready to answer questions later in the day, in our plenary question time.

And so we come to the final speaker of the morning. We have heard some provocative and controversial stuff, but there is yet more to come! For one of the most controversial areas of children and worship is their relationship to the sacraments – baptism and Holy Communion. The issue of baptism has been well-trodden for many decades, if not centuries. To discuss it yet again would add nothing new to the debate about children and worship. But the question of children and Communion is relatively new and focusses many of the issues we have already considered: the role of parents; power in the church; the exclusion of children; faith development. Few of us, however, have thought systematically about the subject. To conclude this session, therefore, I invite Professor Grant Weston from the Practical Theology Department of the University of Stokehampton to speak on the subject of children and Communion.

Grant: I'm grateful to have been invited to speak on a subject that is dear to my heart and which has occupied me for nearly twenty years. Let me begin with a bit of biography.

When I was ordained into the Methodist ministry some years ago after a fairly turbulent life, one of the most difficult things I had to do was to explain to parents and children why the children couldn't take part in the central act of worship – the breaking of bread. I went through the usual run of arguments: that Communion was an essentially adult rite; that it required adult assent to Christian faith; that it presupposed an intellectual ability to discern and judge, which was beyond children; that St Paul had said the elements were not to be taken lightly, irreverently or without understanding; and so on. You know the script.

However, I became increasingly unhappy with this approach. We had offered alternatives: that children should come forward with their parents to the Communion rail for a blessing, for example. But the more I tried to work according to the rules, the less I remained convinced. I found myself turning all sorts of blind eyes to parents who slipped their kids a piece of bread broken off from their own or those who encouraged their children to look at me with eyes wide open as they held out their hands to me for bread.

Then one day it happened. The thing I had dreaded. It was a summer Sunday and we had a new family visiting. I later discovered they were from Australia where the Uniting Church (which includes the Methodists) administers Communion to children. As the parents and their three children came to the rail, I duly gave bread to the adults and began to bless the youngsters. Then, to my horror, the children all requested (sotto voce) the bread and wine. I clamped my hands on their heads, said a quick prayer of blessing and moved on as fast as I could.

Afterwards, I was faced with two upset parents and three puzzled kids. Only then did I realise that they were fully entitled to receive Communion and that my actions had been tantamount to a slap in the face. From that moment on I determined to spend as much time as I could studying the history and theology of children and the sacraments. I enrolled for postgraduate research and spent every spare moment hard at it. The years since then have been spent looking at the theological and practical issues surrounding children and the church.

So, unlike Jeanne Stanley, I come to you as an academic. But like her, I'm motivated by a combination of personal and pastoral experience. My theological work has been the outcome of that. I hope what I bring today in its small way may be helpful to those who are on the same journey.
But now I have shared my autobiography (or at least a bit of it), let me move to the issue I have been asked to speak about: children and Communion.[2]

I want to begin by dividing my material into three sections: Scripture, theology and history. That seems to me the right order in which to tackle the subject. Our starting point needs to be Scripture because it is the final authority for faith and life. It is God's word – his disclosure of himself, his acts in history, his revelation in his Son Jesus and his inspiration of the biblical writers. When we listen to Scripture, we listen to God. What it says, he says.

Theology, on the other hand, is an activity that flows from being confronted by the Word of God. To say that God has spoken in Scripture, and supremely in his Son, takes us so far but we need to go further. We need to reflect upon what Scripture means, we need to relate it to human experience, we need to piece together a coherent way (or ways) of interpreting God's revelation. This is the task of theology.

That, in turn, brings us to history. We live in an age which seems to think that every question it faces has been newly-minted: that no generation has faced such questions before. But even the briefest of glances at history – in our case church history and the history of theology – tells us that almost all questions (in some shape or form) have already been raised and addressed by those who have gone before.

I hope to show today that in all these three areas – Scripture, theology, history – there are good reasons for believing that the admission of children to Holy Communion, far from being the latest fad, can be seen as a reflection of the creative promptings of God's Spirit as he speaks to our age.

Beginning with Scripture, then, what do we find? In the first place, both Old and New Testaments have a positive attitude towards children. They are highly valued. In the Old, they represent the future both for individual families and for the community. As one writer comments: 'They were valued for their potential, as future members of the covenant community (boys) or as guardians of the family and bearers of the next generation (girls).'[3]

In the New Testament we find the same attitude since the first Christians, after all, were either Jews or inherited Jewish ways of thinking. But with the important exception of Jesus' comments in the gospels, children are mentioned only in passing – in the context of Paul's references to household life, for example. So we read in Ephesians 6:1,2, 'Children obey your parents in the Lord, for this is right. Honour your father and mother.' Other references which speak of households imply rather than specify the presence of children.

Does this relative silence suggest that children were excluded from the religious life – and therefore the worship life – of God's people? Certainly this wasn't the case in the Old Testament where the whole community of faith, including its youngest members, were counted as the people of God. They were called to remember God's gracious acts towards them as a nation, and the recollection of such acts formed the centrepiece of worship. Children were reckoned to be part of the worshipping community and participated along with adults. Here is what one Old Testament commentator says:

> Much Old Testament material looks back to the time
> Israelites spent journeying in the wilderness as a time of
> closeness to God, of God's guidance and Israel's
> dependence ... The people of Israel remembered their time
> as a pilgrim people and kept the tradition alive through
> their worship. And in that all the members of the family
> were included, children as well as adults.[4]

When we turn to the early Christian communities of the New Testament, we find they operated with the same outlook but with one important difference: they no longer looked back solely to the acts of God in the Old Testament.

They interpreted all these in the light of the coming of Jesus. His death and resurrection were now the focus of remembering; and worship reflected this. But the Old Testament assumption and practice remained: children were presumed to be members of the community of faith and were present as it celebrated the works of God and looked forward to the pilgrimage being completed when Christ returned. Children were every bit as much a part of worship in the New Testament as in the Old.

So much for the epistles. What about those passages from the Gospels dealing with children? Interestingly, Jesus reflected Jewish attitudes but moved beyond them. He reflected them in that he refused to be sentimental about children. Unlike we moderns, he turned his back on painting an idealised picture of them in such passages as Matthew 11: 16–19 (also found in Luke 7: 31–35) or Mark 10:15. At no point does he say anything about their innocence or inherent goodness as modern writers tend to do. Rather, he uses children to make a different point. He argues that they offer us a model for discipleship because (a) they are receptive; and (b) their openness to receive makes them 'those to whom God gives the Kingdom in an act of free generosity.' To quote once more: 'In the teaching of Jesus itself, children are not, as in Jewish thought, those who are only taught or trained, but those from whom adults can also learn.'[5]

But if we really want to grasp the revolutionary significance of Jesus' teaching, we need to listen to Professor Hans-Reudi Weber:

> …it is the relationship with Jesus which makes these
> children representatives of God. As such they are our
> teachers. In their objective humility and need, they cry
> "mother", "father", "Abba", and they stretch out their
> empty hands. If we want to learn how to receive the
> kingdom and how to become God's representatives, we
> must learn it from the child in our midst.[6]

What makes Jesus' teaching revolutionary, then, is that he ceased to regard children 'simply as objects of education, those who need to be brought and trained for adulthood before they achieve any real significance. Rather they are seen as patterns of discipleship, those who teach as well as learn.'[7] This placed a higher value on them as individuals in their own right than either Jewish society or any of the prevailing cultures around. We shouldn't underestimate how truly revolutionary Jesus was. Children mattered to him, and they mattered big.

There's much more that could be said about the Bible. But we need to move on to look at theology. Here I want to focus on a theology of sacrament as the central issue to which we need to turn our attention.

Firstly, what do we mean by a sacrament? We use the term freely (in some denominations more freely than others) but what does it mean? The generally accepted view since the Reformation has been that *sacraments constitute outward and visible signs of inward, invisible grace*. That's why they can't be regarded as having quasi-magical effects just by participating in them. The acts of being baptised or receiving Holy Communion do not in themselves make us more acceptable to God, more holy or change our lives. Rather, they indicate that God is already at work in us: they are signs of grace, not causes of it.

Now, arising from this definition, it is possible to take two contrary views. The first – what we might call the 'Baptist' view – holds that the sacraments can only be valid for individuals where there has been conscious acceptance and understanding of them. And, moreover, the individual must be capable of giving a reasoned account of this and the change that God has wrought in his or her life. In other words, human response is a vital aspect of the meaning, reality and effectiveness of a sacrament.

The other view, held by Methodists, Anglicans and others, contends that response is not the most important aspect of a sacrament. Instead, this view emphasises God's gracious initiative as the central core of what a sacrament is. If we want to get a true picture of sacraments we must start with grace itself rather than with our response to grace. On this basis, sacraments are signs of God's initiative and his promise held out to us. This is the most fundamental thing about a sacrament. In other words, *they are first and foremost signs of God's action and only secondarily indicators of our response*. If we want to make sense of sacraments, we must begin with God and not with ourselves.

We are presented, then, with two contrasting approaches that have radically different implications for children. If we take the 'Baptist' view, we shall reckon that neither baptism nor Communion is appropriate for children. They must wait until individuals are able to make an adult-style profession of faith to show that their lives really have been touched by God and that he has accomplished a saving and sanctifying work within them.

The alternative view offers a rather different outcome. If the emphasis lies in what God has done and is doing, the possibility of children receiving sacraments becomes much more real. All that is needed to receive the signs of God's promise is faith. Intellectual understanding, emotional and spiritual maturity are entirely secondary. As long as faith is operative, the way is open to receive the sacraments as tokens of God's love and grace.

And since it becomes a matter of faith, receiving them does not depend upon the capacities of the receiver. Making tests or hurdles which children have to jump in order to qualify as genuine believers flies in the face of a gospel of grace. To do so is to resurrect a doctrine of salvation by human efforts rather than by free grace received through faith.

This is the heart of the theological argument for the admission of children to Communion (to baptism as well, for that matter). But at what point does faith come in? Are we not in danger of reverting to the pre-Reformation position whereby the mere reception of the sacraments was enough to guarantee salvation?

The answer to this must be no, since faith in Christ is still the key. And this is where faith development theorists have brought something new to the debate. For if faith development suggests anything, it is that *faith must not be defined by intellectual categories alone or by reaching a supposed 'age of discretion or understanding'*. Rather, faith has to be defined in a much more subtle, nuanced and complex way according to the characteristics of each faith stage. It's not a matter of giving assent to a number of doctrinal beliefs and being able to articulate how they affect our lives. That is all very cognitive and, if I may say so, middle class. It presupposes levels and modes of thinking and articulation that are culturally-conditioned according to the educated West. Feminist critics might also add that such an approach is heavily masculine.

But if faith has to do with a mode of being rather than a way of thinking – in other words, having an openness to relationship with Christ – it follows that such a possibility is present in all stages of faith. The form it takes will be different according to whatever stage a child may occupy. In earlier stages, the cognitive or intellectual aspect will be minimised or even absent altogether. In later ones it will play a greater part. The important point is that faith development studies enable us to adopt a much more nuanced approach to the admission of children to the sacraments than the way the argument is usually conducted. We can appreciate that there is no magic age or threshold at which children enter into saving faith. Rather, we are all on a continuum of faith from the day we are born. We respond to what we know and understand of God according to the stage we have reached on this continuum.

I would close this section by making one further point. The New Testament sees baptism and Communion as the signs of entry into and membership of the kingdom of God. But if children are excluded from either or both, what does this say about their status as children of God? If the sacraments are to be withheld from them simply because they are children, does that mean they are outside the kingdom?

I would suggest that most of us would hold back from such a conclusion with all the implications it contains. We would want to affirm that children in the church of the twenty-first century are members of the people of God, as were children in the nation of Israel or the churches of the New Testament. Here, no test of belief was put forward and the rule was to include them in all aspects of the worship of the believing community rather than exclude them solely on the grounds that they were children. Theological considerations offer no support for denying children the sacraments any more than does the evidence of Scripture.

So much for Scripture and theology. That leaves us with the experience of the church in history. What does this tell us? As the title of my paper is 'Children and Holy Communion', I propose not to deal with the subject of infant baptism which has been well-analysed elsewhere. The subject of child Communion has been less well documented.

Interestingly, we find references to children receiving Communion as early as the third century AD. Cyprian of Carthage, who died in 258, tells a story of a little girl whose nurse had taken her to a pagan ritual without the parents' knowledge. When she returned and was taken to church by her mother, she was fractious and disturbed. When offered the Communion cup (note!) she refused but the minister persisted. At this point she vomited. Cyprian goes on to say that she was too young to tell her parents that she had been taken to a pagan ritual. Indeed, the fact that she had a nurse underlines this point.

Now what is significant about this tale is that Cyprian clearly regarded it as quite normal for a child of that age to receive Communion. There is no hint that he (or his contemporaries) thought it odd or wrong. The little girl is not adduced as an example of inadmissibility but of precisely the opposite: that children should receive Communion but that parents have a responsibility to watch over their spiritual preparation. So if any of you have childminders or nannies, the moral is clear: keep them away from pagan celebrations!

Cyprian is also interesting because elsewhere he refers to children having been accustomed to receiving Communion from birth, or, as he puts it, 'in the arms of their parents' from 'the very beginning of their nativity.'[8] This is not an argument I wish to pursue here but it's worth noting that the early church apparently found it impossible to impose an arbitrary age threshold and therefore admitted children to Communion from the moment they were born, as does the Orthodox Church today.

When we turn to the fourth century, we find that yet more witnesses recorded – in passing rather than as a matter for debate – the fact of child Communion. A Syrian document called the *Apostolic Constitutions* stipulated the order of precedence in which members of a congregation were to receive Communion. Significantly, children were to come forward after the church leaders but before the rest of the congregation along with the deaconesses, virgins and widows. The men came last!

From the same period we also have a story of a funeral inscription from

Sicily, commemorating a small girl, Julia Florentina, who was taken ill when she was about eighteen months old. At the request of her parents, she received baptism and Communion prior to her death. Both sacraments were regarded as normal practice.

Our final witness in this period, however, is none other than that theological giant St Augustine. At the end of the fourth century he took his more familiar (to us) doctrine of inborn sinfulness, or original sin as it's perhaps better known, and turned it on its head. We might have expected him to argue that since children were sinful (like all human beings) from birth, they would be ineligible to receive Communion. But exactly the opposite is the case. For Augustine, the spiritual helplessness of children meant that they stand in need of grace (symbolised in the sacraments) just as much as adults. Taking the text John 6:53, ('Unless you eat the flesh of the Son of man and drink his blood, how can you have life within you?'), Augustine developed this into a case for the inclusion of children in Communion. Otherwise, how could they be saved? It's not an argument I would myself deploy but Augustine thought differently. The point was that child Communion was already happening and Augustine sought to offer an additional theological support for it.

We see, then that there's clear evidence for admission of children to Communion in the early church. But what of later centuries?

Throughout the early Middle Ages, children continued to receive Communion; and as late as the reign of Pope Paschal II (1099–1118) regulations were issued conceding that if young children found it difficult to digest wine and bread separately, they should have the bread dipped in the wine. However, within a hundred years, the trend towards restriction had resulted in Bishop Odo of Paris in 1175 advising that children were to be refused consecrated bread and could drink only the wine rinsed out of the cup after Communion had been administered. Finally in 1215, children throughout the church were excluded completely from taking bread or wine before the age of discretion, set at seven and then pushed back to twelve or fourteen.

The late Middle Ages, then, saw a reversal of the policy that had applied from the early church onwards as an increased reverence for the sacrament restricted access to it. This became true even for adults. The same set of regulations that excluded children in 1215 also put a figure on the number of times adults should take Communion per year – at least once. This became a ruling that rapidly turned from a minimum into a maximum. For the vast majority, Communion became an annual event. As William Strange has noted, 'The reverence for the sacrament in the later Middle Ages was such that reception had become virtually a privilege of the priesthood.'[9]

But that's not quite the end of the story. In the early fifteenth century, under the impact of a reformation (not *the* Reformation, by the way) in Bohemia, the Hussite movement incorporated infant Communion into its articles of faith. They were determined that ' the poor, the weak and the children should not be excluded from the community's central act of worship.'[10] Later, the Reformation churches chose to continue the practice of exclusion advocated by the Council of 1215 (though not the theology put forward to justify it). There was some debate in England among the Puritans in the seventeenth century and the case for readmitting children seemed to have been won, but politics intervened and nothing changed.

And so the position has remained until our own times. Following studies initiated by the international Lambeth Conference of Bishops in 1958, a number of branches of Anglicanism had, by the early 1970s, come round to admitting children to Communion. The USA, Canada, New Zealand and Australia are among the list. In 1999, the Church of England did the same. And other denominations such as the Uniting Church of Australia have followed suit. In doing so, they looked back to the three sources we have discussed today: Scripture, theology and history. I'm glad to say they found in all of them a convergence of reasons for change.

Chair: Thank you Professor Weston for a very thorough and fascinating survey. I have already been notified of a flood of questions that conference members wish to ask and if we were to take even three quarters of them we would require another hour at least. Grant has therefore kindly agreed to respond to questions in an extra session after lunch. In the meantime, I have allowed just a few questions to whet our appetites.

Questioner: I found your talk riveting since I was not aware of the evidence you have collected together. But one point continues to trouble me. I don't know whether it comes in the Scripture or the theology section but it is this: in 1 Corinthians 11: 27–29, St Paul speaks of the need to examine ourselves prior to eating and drinking bread and wine, otherwise, to use his words, 'whoever eats the bread or drinks the cup of the Lord in an unworthy manner will be guilty of sinning against the body and blood of the Lord.' Surely this kind of self-examination is something that can only be done by adults?

Grant: The short answer is: only if you think Paul is talking about intellectual self-examination. But the passage suggests that he has in mind something else, namely the self-indulgence surrounding the Lord's table that he refers to only a few verses before (20,21). Apparently, the Corinthians were insulting the meaning of the meal by treating it as an opportunity for greed and gluttony. This may also have been connected with competitive factionalism (vs 17–19). In short, they were abusing the privilege of Communion. This was not an intellectual matter but a moral one. In exhorting them to examine themselves, Paul was not speaking of being able to give assent to a basis of faith but of behaving themselves properly.

Now when we apply this principle to children we can see that it is perfectly appropriate to require all ages to make sure they are in a right relationship with God and other people and that they are treating the occasion with due reverence. These are matters that cut across ages and faith stages.

Questioner: But surely individuals have to be able to understand what Communion is all about before they're allowed to take it?

Grant: Yes, but the question is: what do we mean by understanding? I've already argued that to think of this as purely doctrinal or intellectual understanding is misplaced. If we were to make the articulation of certain doctrines a test, what would we do about those who have learning difficulties? Would we exclude them on the grounds that they were unable to pass the test? Surely not. In those cases we would (I hope) say that they were just as capable of receiving the love and grace of God as the next person, irrespective of intellectual capacity. What's more, any doctrinal test that supposedly indicated whether grace was at work would run into all sorts of problems: who would decide what to include, for example? And who would have the right to make the decision? What would be the acceptable level of explanation or articulation on the part of the applicant, and how would we tell whether they really had experienced the grace of God? It all comes rather close to the kind of judging and pronouncing on others that Jesus warns against.

Questioner: Despite the impressive array of material you have assembled, Professor, I can't help feeling such a radical change as you advocate would fly in the face of the overwhelming tradition of the church. I suppose what I'm saying is that the evidence you cite seems a bit thin for the change you're proposing.

Grant: The test, of course, is whether any proposed change can be shown to be a denial of Scripturally-based theology. If I thought that the admission of children to Communion represented such a denial, I would be the first to disown it. But, for the reasons I have set out, I don't.

The second thing I would say is that theologically, Communion is an act that looks forward as well as backward. True, it recalls to us the death of Christ (past event) but it also anticipates his return (future event). What's more, it foreshadows another meal, the marriage supper of the Lamb in Revelation, when all the people of God will celebrate in heaven. Now I ask you this: can we really conceive of that heavenly meal taking place without children? And if not, is it theologically acceptable that we should exclude them from the Church's central meal on earth that is a foretaste of heaven?

(*At this point, the conference adjourned and the transcript ends.*)

Notes to appendix 1

1   See, for example, Peter Graystone and Elaine Turner, *A Church for All Ages: A Practical Approach to All-Age Worship*, London, Scripture Union 1993; A Barton, *All-Age Worship*, Cambridge, Grove Books, 1993 for useful discussions of the 'how to' issues.

2   For further reading on the subject of children and Communion from a theological and historical perspective, see the following: WA Strange, *Children in the Early Church*, Carlisle, Paternoster 1996, pp103–9. This book also contains useful chapters on children in the ancient world and in the New Testament. Also, David Holeton, *Infant Communion Then and Now*, Nottingham, Grove Books 1981. On children and the Bible in general, see The Church of England's General Synod Board of Education report *Children in the Way*, London, National Society/Church House Publishing 1988, chapter 6.

3   *Children in the Way*, p72. Extracts are copyright © The National Society and are reproduced by permission.

4   *Children in the Way*, pp75–6.

5   *Children in the Way*, p74.

6   *Children in the Way*, p74.

7   *Children in the Way*, p74.

8   WA Strange, *Children in the Early Church*, Carlisle, Paternoster 1996, p105.

9   Strange, p107.

10   Strange, p108.

Appendix 2: Children and spiritual gifts

'Do not quench the Spirit,' said Paul to the Thessalonian Christians, twenty years after Christ's death (1 Thessalonians 5:19; RSV). Two thousand years later, there are many millions of people touched by the renewal movement for whom this text has become a watchword. When Anglican bishops are publicly seen to dance in the Spirit, we know something has happened! What started out in modern times as a trickle at the edges of the church's life has turned into a mighty river sweeping through its core.

But the debate has moved on to a new stage. The theology as well as the fact of spiritual gifts (charismata) has been widely accepted by many and the practices of speaking in tongues, interpretation, prophecy and other gifts mentioned by Paul are no longer dismissed as the unbalanced enthusiasm of a few cranks and weirdos. Many churches have incorporated them into their life and worship.

In the mainstream denominations this has been confined largely to adults. Now further questions are being asked: are spiritual gifts for children too? Should we encourage youngsters to seek and receive them?[1] More specifically, should evangelism include an exhortation to seek charismata as well as salvation?

In the discussion that follows, we shall be thinking mainly of the more inspirational and public gifts listed in 1 Corinthians 12:27–30, such as tongues, prophecy, healing and interpretation. These are highly-charged theologically and emotionally, and for the reasons I shall give are (I believe) normally inappropriate for children. Other gifts, less susceptible to emotional manipulation, such as helping and leadership (v 28) and those similarly listed in Romans 12:7,8, such as generosity and compassion are gifts that should be encouraged. When I speak, therefore, of spiritual gifts as inappropriate I refer to the inspirational/public kind rather than the others. Tongues, prophecy, etc might not be appropriate in the light of child and faith development theory and theology outlined in this book, but helping, generosity, compassion and so on, most surely are.

The case for encouraging children to receive the Spirit's gifts might run something like this:

1. The gifts are Spirit-given blessings to the people of God. Children count as God's people no less than adults. The gifts are therefore intended for both children and adults.
2. Spiritual gifts are part of the experience of belonging to Christ and being 'in him'. Jesus said that children belonged to him and rebuked those who tried to stop children from reaching him. This surely means that they are inheritors of his blessings. These include spiritual gifts.
3. All Christians receive the Holy Spirit when they receive Christ. When children receive Christ, they likewise receive the Spirit, which means receiving his gifts too.
4. If children are capable of receiving the gift of salvation, they are capable also of receiving gifts of the Spirit.

There is a certain coherence about these arguments: they seem to make a great deal of sense. But is that really the case? How do we go about evaluating them? The issue is so controversial that we cannot avoid having to engage in some tough theological reasoning.

We shall look principally at New Testament discussion of spiritual gifts to see if we can find any clues which will help us in our quest. The kind of questions we shall be concerned with include: What is the nature of spiritual gifts? What is their purpose? Does their character mean that they are intended only for adults or could we envisage the New Testament sanctioning their use by children? Are there any explicit principles which would either forbid or encourage children to exercise them?

These are large questions. But they must be set alongside insights afforded by the study of child development. If we accept that every person goes through stages of faith which are related to physical, social and psychological development, how do these fit with either the experience of charismata or a theology of gifts? The New Testament must be our basic resource for answering theological questions and must be the final authority in matters of faith, but we must also ask how theology and experience relate to what we know about human growth and development.

There is also a third area that we cannot afford to ignore. In the years since the first edition of *Children Finding Faith,* we have become much more aware of the fact of child abuse. High-profile cases brought to light by the media, along with further research into how children have been treated both in institutional and domestic contexts reveal a disturbing story. At its worst, this has included horrific sexual exploitation of children in all age groups from infants to teenagers, and unfortunately the church has not been exempt from such acts. But at a less dramatic level, we have been alerted to the potential for manipulation and exploitation that is present in all adult-child relationships. Having considered the theological and developmental aspects, therefore, we shall need to reflect upon the implications of society's current wariness about those who work with children. This should make us doubly conscious of the need to tread very carefully indeed for the sake both of children and of public perceptions of the Church's ministry to children.

Insights from the New Testament

The New Testament as a whole is not very much concerned with spiritual gifts. Most of its teaching on the subject can be found in the writings of Paul, notably chapters twelve to fourteen of his first letter to the Corinthians. It is here that we find a detailed theology which furnishes some guidelines for the use of gifts in the church.

It is interesting to reflect how much we would know about charismata if Corinth had not been a problem congregation. Paul's discussion of gifts does not take the form of abstract theological proportions but a series of points to deal with specific difficulties. What we have, then, is not so much a prospectus for a maker's manual about how to develop spiritual gifts, but a number of responses to a particularly complex situation. This should caution us against reading Paul's comments as a set of rules which can be simply lifted out of the context for which they were written and plonked down upon a late twentieth century church in a very different situation. Nevertheless, once we have got this fact into our heads, it becomes possible to trace continuities between Corinth and ourselves so that we can at least find some clues to aid us in our search. The first task must be for us to reconstruct, as far as possible, the context of Paul's writing.

What kind of church existed at Corinth?

Corinth was a great sea port. It controlled the land route from north to south and the sea route from east to west. It was a bustling city full of corruption. Its reputation for immorality went back a century and had been so great that it spawned a new word for excess and sexual licence: to Corinthianise.

Christians converted from paganism had to resist not only the city's corruption but the effects of pagan worship. Sacrifices to idols were commonplace and the town was dominated by the temple of Aphrodite, the goddess of love, with her thousands of temple prostitutes.

It is little wonder, then, that the church at Corinth was beset with problems. In the course of his first letter, we find Paul dealing with: divisions, factions and party jealousies (1:11–13) with some members taking others to court; immorality even between Christians and prostitutes (6:15–20); disputes over food offered to idols (8:1–13); gluttony at the Lord's Supper at which people guzzled the bread and wine like animals (11:17–22); chaos in worship (14:33); lack of love (13:1–13); denial of Christ's resurrection (15:12); and questioning of Paul's apostleship (4:1–3,15; 9:1,2). In short, the Corinthian church was an unholy, unspiritual mess.

This was the context in which spiritual gifts were operating. It is worth noting that Paul does not deny the validity of such gifts on the grounds of the church's unspirituality. He does not say that such people could never exercise gifts. After all, Paul has laid the foundation of the Corinthian church (3:10) and knew that despite the problems there remained a genuineness of faith. As C K Barrett comments: 'He neither denies the right of such phenomena to exist within the church nor affirms that in themselves they are proof of the presence and activity of the Spirit of God.'[2]

But this does not mean that Paul uncritically accepted every claim to a spiritual gift simply because someone felt the Spirit come upon them. He calls instead for a mature discernment of the true from the false. The key to this, he reminds his readers, is the relationship between the believer and Christ.

'Now about spiritual gifts, brothers, I do not want you to be ignorant ... no-one can say, "Jesus is Lord," except by the Holy Spirit' (1 Corinthians 12:1,3).

What Paul is *not* saying is that the mere formula 'Jesus is Lord' shows a person's true obedience to Christ – anybody can parrot the words.

Rather, the life of the Christian who claims to possess a gift reflects his submission to the lordship of Jesus in all its spiritual and ethical dimensions. Only when accompanied by a life of genuine Christ-likeness, should a gift be counted as authentically inspired by God's Spirit. As Barrett comments:

'The true Christian watchword is Jesus is Lord ... It is true not because it is the right or orthodox formula but because it expresses the proper relationship with Jesus: the speaker accepts his authority and proclaims himself the servant of him whom he confesses as Lord.'[3]

The Corinthians have to recognise, therefore, that some of their gifts may be counterfeit and that merely claiming to speak under the inspiration of the Spirit is not enough. The reason for Paul's caution is that ecstatic gifts, especially tongues, were part and parcel of pagan worship. Some of the Christians in Corinth who had been converted from paganism may well have exercised pagan spiritual gifts in their former religion. Paul is concerned, therefore, to urge the Corinthians not to accept claims to inspiration uncritically, but to assess whatever is said or done by a number of simple tests. This is what lies behind his statement: 'You know when you were heathen you were led astray to dumb idols, however you may have been moved' (12:2; RSV). It was possible for a person to exercise what appeared to be a spiritual gift and yet be acting not according to the Spirit of God but out of a hangover from pagan days or at the promptings of the Deceiver.

The tests of authenticity

For Paul, then, feelings were not the decisive evidence of authenticity. The person who claimed to possess a gift of the Spirit must be willing to submit to a fourfold test:

1. *The lives of believers must be consistent* with their claims to be led by God. Paul was not looking for perfection but for evidence of the fruits as well as the gifts of the Spirit. There must be a match between the attitudes and lives of believers on one hand and their alleged gifts on the other. The key to this was love. Christians who claimed a gift such as tongues or prophecy, for example, but whose lives demonstrated a lack of love either did not possess the genuine article or needed further teaching. Either way, they would be insensitive and brash like a gong or a clanging cymbal (13:1) – however eloquent they might be.

We can see this point worked out in detail in Paul's letters to the Ephesians and the Galatians. In both places (Ephesians 4 and 5; Galatians 5), he stresses that to live in the Spirit doesn't just mean experiencing the gifts of the Spirit but also entails the fruit of the Spirit. The characteristics of a fruit-filled life are love, joy, peace, patience, kindness, goodness, faithfulness, gentleness, self-control (Galatians 5:22,23), combined with lowliness, meekness, bearing with one another, and eagerness to maintain the unity of the Spirit in the bond of peace (Ephesians 4:1–3).

These are all the fruits of maturity. They are not optional extras but the evidence of authentic Christian experience. Paul is well aware that they are not fruits which can grow overnight but nevertheless he is insistent that those who claim the Spirit must show the fruits as well as the gifts if their claim is to be taken seriously.

2. *The content of a gift must conform to Christian truth.* Hence, 'no-one who is speaking by the Spirit of God says, "Jesus be cursed" (1 Corinthians 12:3). Significantly, elsewhere in the New Testament we find similar tests (1 John 4:1–3).

3. *A gift must edify or build up the church.* We shall deal with this in more detail later.

4. *A gift must be evaluated by others in the church* (1 Corinthians 14:29). There are three possible meanings of this verse:
(a) a gift should be assessed by those who possess the same gift (prophets should test prophecy, healers healings, etc);
(b) a gift should be tested by the general leadership of the church;
(c) a gift should be tested by the congregation as a whole.

It is not clear from the text which of these Paul had in mind, but the underlying point remains: gifts should be tested by mature, responsible members of the church and not just accepted on the say-so of the claimant. This is a crucial point of pastoral practice.

The situation at Corinth, then, was complex and peculiar. Side by side with immorality, false teaching and unspirituality we find spiritual gifts. This leads us to ask a second question.

What kind of people should exercise gifts?

In Paul's view, the only people whose claims to possess spiritual gifts should be taken seriously are those whose lives are ethically and spiritually mature. It is here that we find an illuminating reference by the apostle to the place of children. In 1 Corinthians 14:20, Paul likens the spiritual immaturity of the Corinthians to the natural immaturity of children:

'Brothers, stop thinking like children. In regard to evil be infants, but in your thinking be adults.'

The significance of this verse is that it appears in the middle of Paul's discussion of the conditions required for the legitimate exercise of charismata. By comparing the Corinthians with children, he is saying that by nature children are immature. But the Corinthians are not to be like children in their practice of spiritual gifts – they are to show adult maturity. This alone is fitting.

The contrast Paul makes between children and maturity suggests that children are too immature, in general, to exercise those gifts of the Spirit which I have identified earlier as inappropriate. Of course, there may be exceptions, but the maturity required for the proper use of charismata is an essentially adult quality. If this is not an implication of 14:20, it is difficult to see what is.

What Paul means by immaturity can be seen from his earlier comments in chapter 3. He had used the image of childhood as a warning to his readers:

'Brothers, I could not address you as spiritual but as
worldly - mere infants in Christ. I gave you milk not solid
food, for you were not yet ready for it. Indeed, you are still
not ready. You are still worldly. For since there is jealousy
and quarrelling among you, are you not worldly? Are you
not acting like mere men?' (1 Corinthians 3:1–3)

Immaturity, then is the failure to live ethically, to recognise that the lordship of Christ requires a new way of living. Maturity, on the other hand, is reflected in a genuinely Christ-like humility and love. This, in turn, requires an adult understanding of the death and resurrection of Christ, the significance of the Spirit and the meaning of the Scriptures.

All this presupposes adult capabilities. This is not to say that children cannot trust in Christ or know the work of his Spirit in their lives. But this will be at a level appropriate to the natural immaturity of the child years.

The possession and use of spiritual gifts, argues Paul, must be accompanied by a mature demonstration of fruits of the Spirit. Taken together, they presuppose a maturity which lies beyond the capabilities of childhood.

What are the gifts for?

In his dialogue with the Corinthians, Paul tackles two common but mistaken notions of the purpose of charismata. We need to take note of what he says because they are used today to justify the seeking of spiritual gifts both for children and adults.

Mistake number one: Charismata are given to prove the presence of God to unbelievers.

This view is widespread, especially in relation to healing. 'Signs and wonders' ministry in particular assumes that spectacular manifestations of supernatural power will convince the unbeliever of the truth of the gospel and drive him to faith. Urging us to see this as normative for evangelism today, John Wimber writes that, 'through these supernatural encounters people experience the presence and power of God ... resistance to the gospel is supernaturally overcome and receptivity to Christ's claims is usually very high.'[4]

This is not the place to discuss the theology of power evangelism in detail; but if it is true that the primary purpose of charismata is evangelistic then we can see how their use with children might be defended. However, while we must accept that God in his grace does speak to unbelievers through the use of spiritual gifts, we must also recognise that a careful reading of 1 Corinthians 12 and 14 should make us cautious before we promote them as normal evangelistic tools. Let's spell this out.

Nowhere in either chapter does Paul suggest that the primary purpose of gifts is evangelism. The two gifts he does discuss, because of their effect on unbelievers, are tongues and prophecy. But even here, he says their results will be contradictory. If outsiders hear tongues in worship, they will be confirmed in their unbelief: 'will they not say that you are out of your mind?' (14:23). If they hear prophecy, they will be convicted and turn to God: 'he will fall down and worship God, exclaiming "God is really among you!"' (14:25).

This is the closest Paul comes to an evangelistic interpretation of spiritual gifts. But even so, it is mighty thin ice to skate on. It will not bear the weight put upon it by the signs and wonders school for two reasons.

Firstly, although Paul notes that prophecy can convince unbelievers of God's presence, he does not argue for it as a normative evangelistic weapon. His aim is something quite different: it is to show the Corinthians who were hooked on tongues and prophecy that, of the two, prophecy was more desirable because it was more intelligible. Significantly, he states in 14:19 (RSV) that he 'would rather speak five words with my mind in order to instruct others, than ten thousand words in a tongue.' When Paul says that prophecy convinces outsiders, therefore, he is not advocating its use as a means of witness: he is simply trying to steer the Corinthians away from their obsession with tongues. 'If you must place such heavy reliance on charismata,' he is saying, 'then promote prophecy rather than tongues because at least it can be understood.' This is a far cry from advocating it as part of a programme of power evangelism.

Secondly, the overwhelming burden of Paul's teaching in Corinthians is concerned not with soul-winning but with building up the church. This points to a further false idea about spiritual gifts.

Mistake number two: Gifts are primarily for personal enjoyment; they carry the believer into a new stage of spiritual life where his or her walk with God and spirituality are deepened and enriched.

The essential error in this view is that it mistakes the by-product of a gift (personal enjoyment by the possessor) for the fundamental purpose (edification of the whole body of Christ). Paul is adamant that gifts are given for the good of the church rather than the benefit of the possessor: 'to each one the manifestation of the Spirit is given *for the common good'* (12:7). 'Since you are eager to have spiritual gifts, try to excel in gifts that *build up the church'* (14:12).

Paul underlines his point by explaining the purpose of the gift of tongues. These are important, he contends, but they must always be used so that others may be built up. They are not simply for private consumption. It is no good babbling away in unintelligible noises just for your own sake. Such an activity may make you feel good but it runs counter to the basic reason for which gifts were given: the edification of others. At the very least, the tongue-speaker in worship should pray for an interpretation (14:13) but if there is no recognised interpreter in the congregation the gift should not be used (14:28). Even better (says Paul) let tongues give way to prophecy which can be understood by all.

These may seem harsh words but in the muddled and unbalanced context of Corinth they were necessary. Paul's purpose is to see that the gifts of the Spirit are used for the benefit of all and not just a few.

What does he mean when he speaks of building up or edification? Paul has in mind two kinds of Christians: (a) those who claim gifts in order to indulge and draw attention to themselves ('Look how great I am, I speak in tongues'); and (b) those whose gifts point the onlooker away from the user to God or to the needs of others. Gifts which edify are those which achieve the latter purpose: they encourage, strengthen and challenge. They are not part of an ego-trip.

How is this to be achieved? Paul gives his answer by contrasting tongues with prophecy. The Corinthians had elevated tongues to the supreme place among charismata. Unless you spoke in tongues you could not be regarded as spiritual. Paul turns this view on its head, first by putting tongues at the end, not the beginning, of his list of gifts in chapter 12; and second, by comparing them to prophecy.

Prophecy is portrayed as an example of the true purpose of gifts because 'everyone who prophesies speaks to men for their strengthening, encouragement and comfort. He who speaks in a tongue edifies himself but he who prophesies edifies the church' (14:3,4). The superiority of prophecy lies, therefore, in its capacity to benefit the whole church and not just the one who utters it. Moreover, it serves as the model for other gifts: they should all aim at mutual upbuilding. 'Since you are eager to have spiritual gifts, try to excel in gifts that build up the church' (14:12). These words addressed to the early Christians also address us today.

What about children?

How does all this relate to children? We have to remember what gifts are and are not for. We have already seen that their purpose is neither to impress non-Christians nor to boost the possessor. So it is no good arguing for children to seek them on the grounds that gifts will convert them to Christ or deepen their walk with God. For reasons which will become clear when we consider insights from child development, pushing children to receive charismata is more likely to produce long-term spiritual casualties than long-term spiritual fruit. If we have been entrusted with the spiritual and psychological well-being of young people, we must not play fast and loose with their hearts and minds simply to satisfy our own theological or spiritual egos.

Once we grasp the logic of Paul's argument, we have a major problem with the view that children should be encouraged to seek the vocal/inspirational gifts of the Spirit. The maturity of mind and spirit which a proper exercise of the gifts presupposes, is only rarely to be found in children.

The alternative is to hold a 'hosepipe' view of inspiration. According to this, the possessor of a gift is entirely passive in the operation of the gift. God simply channels his power through him rather like a gardener channels water from the tap to the garden via the home. In neither case does the channel have anything to do with what goes through it. It is no more than a passive instrument.

This is the idea many Christians hold of charismata: the believer is a conduit for the power of God rather than a creative partner with whom God has chosen to work. If this were true, it could be argued that children can just as easily be channels for divine inspiration as adults. But this proves too much: if inspiration is simply a matter of being a spiritual hosepipe why should we limit the use of gifts to children? Why not animals, on the precedent of Balaam's ass?

This is not the nature of inspiration. Thinking that it was led the Corinthians to elevate tongues above everything else. But Paul's emphasis on the use of the mind and his preference for prophecy were designed to make clear that the exercise of spiritual gifts was not a matter of empty passivity. The gifts are controllable by their possessors and subject to their wills. That is why Paul can tell his audience that if there is no interpreter present in worship, the tongue-speaker should keep quiet *no matter how moved he might feel* (14:28). Similarly, he affirms that 'the spirits of the prophets are subject to the control of prophets' (14:32).

Gifts in the context of worship

There remains one final point which is relevant to children. The only systematic New Testament teaching on spiritual gifts sets them in a particular context: the worship of God's people. The only structure which Paul recognises for the regular use of charismata is the organised worship of the Body of Christ. In Paul's theology, it is the people of God gathered for worship who are the expression of Christ's body. It is through the life of God's people in the fellowship of the local church that the Spirit ministers. This is why Paul gives rules for the conduct of worship and specifies God-given orders of ministry, in which those who possess spiritual gifts are included (12:28). The normal place for the exercise of gifts must be the church under the oversight of recognised spiritual leaders.

Now this is exactly what children's missions, Sunday schools and weekday clubs are not. They have neither the cross-section of age or experience that Paul presupposes in the church, nor do they have the maturity. Their purpose and leadership are entirely different from those of a church. If you are going to argue for child tongue-speakers, prophets and healers, then you will also have to argue for child apostles, teachers, pastors, administrators and so on. In Paul's mind they are inseparable. It is from those who possess spiritual gifts that leadership must arise for there is an intimate connection between the two. And although the New Testament assumes children to be part of the worshipping people of God, it does not reckon them to occupy positions of leadership.

The theological case for encouraging children to seek and exercise charismata, then, is full of problems: it cannot be found at all in the New Testament; its absence from the only systematic teaching we have on gifts is glaring; it conflicts with the nature and purpose of gifts; it overlooks the need for maturity which lies beyond children; it cannot be easily reconciled with a biblical understanding of leadership within the church. Given these considerable problems I believe that it is difficult to mount a convincing case for the practice of child-centred spiritual gifts of the public, inspirational kind (although I am aware that many would do so).

Insights from child development

Whichever model of child development we take, it is clear that adult maturity does not begin to emerge until late adolescence. It may well be that Paul grasped intuitively what we can now show scientifically: that to encourage children to seek and exercise certain spiritual gifts is inappropriate to the general sequence of growth and development. Of course, there may be exceptions as God chooses to fill a child with the Spirit for a particular purpose. But this is not the same thing as supposing that it is

God's *general* will for all children. There are four specific areas which point to the inappropriateness of a child's exercise of spiritual gifts.

1. *Magic*

It is not a great step from seeing spectacular supernatural gifts as the hand of God to thinking of them as magic. This can be particularly true of healings where *the healer* seems to possess untold powers which he can summon up at will by the recitation of a formula which sounds suspiciously like a spell. Such a confusion (which is not unknown among adults) is characteristic, as we have seen, of the junior years. And although it may be acceptable to risk misunderstanding in the context of a child's personal faith-journey in the way I have argued in chapters 3 and 4, it is not acceptable to do so where public ministry is concerned. Children are prone to interpret any spiritual gift as magical simply because the intellectual, emotional and spiritual framework that enables a mature understanding to take place is not yet present. The child inevitably thinks in magical categories. An evangelist or Christian worker who exhorts a child to receive and practice a spiritual gift, therefore, must be aware that he or she is playing with fire. Children are led into all kinds of theological, spiritual and psychological problem areas.

2. *Emotional disturbance*

This is arguably the most dangerous of the problem areas mentioned above. Childhood and adolescence are periods of rapid emotional growth but they are also the periods of greatest turmoil and confusion as the child struggles to find meaning, identity and security. It is easy to exploit this vulnerability, wittingly or unwittingly, by pushing spiritual gifts. Their very nature – dramatic, powerful, supernatural – is immensely appealing. But without an accompanying maturity, they can be enormously disruptive of stable emotional development. At the very worst, particularly in mass meetings, they can be vehicles for manipulation. Exhortations, therefore, to be 'slain in the Spirit' and other so-called spiritual acts are irresponsible and potentially damaging. In any other context they might well be regarded as scandalous. Those who defiantly promote such activities may have much to answer for in later years of development.

A related point is that of authority and responsibility. In a church setting, the minister has a recognised authority. He or she is chosen for (among other things) the gifts of wisdom and maturity. He or she holds authority by virtue of being a recognised leader and is appointed to carry ultimate responsibility for actions which take place within the church. Moreover, if they are a good minister, they will know their congregation (including the children) and will be in a position to evaluate their needs.

In a mission or similar setting, however, the situation is different. Leaders will know very little about the children they meet and will almost certainly not have any ongoing responsibility for them. This can give rise to a great temptation to 'play God' and encourage attitudes and reactions among children which would be unacceptable in a regular church context. The general rule should be: when on mission, encourage only those reactions and consequences for which both you and the host church would be prepared to take responsibility and be accountable for in an ongoing church situation. If neither you nor they would do it as a part of regular ministry, don't do it!

3. Intellectual understanding

Much contemporary research suggests that children may not be capable of the necessary acts of understanding and control of spiritual gifts except in rare cases. 'Speaking with the mind' involves knowing how to relate a gift to the truth about Christ; handling scripture in a mature way; and the capacity to speak words that strengthen, encourage and comfort the hearer. We must say, once more, that from a developmental point of view, these abilities are not present until the onset of adulthood. This is not the same as saying that the gifts are only for intellectuals (God forbid!) but there must be a basic level of adult understanding and maturity.

Exercising Adult Power

To a child, adults are like gods: their word is authoritative and their actions all-powerful. The adult who promotes spiritual gifts, therefore, must realise what she is doing: she, the knowledgeable, unchallengeable authority-figure is saying, either implicitly or explicitly, that the child's Christian experience will not be complete until he has sought these things. But the adult is also saying something else: that *she*, the leader, wants the child to seek a spiritual gift. The child will understand from this that if he is to please the adult, he will do what she says.

It is but a short step to manufacture the required phenomenon. It is a well-known fact (I have experienced it myself) that adolescents can produce tongues or some other kind of inspired utterance in order to please a youth leader or pastor. We should not fool ourselves and should consequently refrain from putting children and adolescents under such pressure.

There is another factor, however. Junior and adolescent youngsters are great peer group affiliators (Westerhoff) and conformists (Fowler). If one member of a group appears to receive a gift, others will soon follow. This is inevitable. But it can lead to delusions of revival as leaders begin to think that a spiritual revolution is under way. More often than not, it is simply another example of the affiliative stage and should be treated in a low-key manner.

So where does that leave us? In my view, given the scale of social concern about the need to respect and protect children, we should err on the side of caution. It is better never to run the risk of being accused of child abuse (and I don't mean sexual abuse alone), than to leave oneself and the church open to the charge in any shape or form. The gospel is too important.

Conclusion

I have argued in favour of spiritual gifts – especially of the less dramatic kind – but for a cautious approach to the promotion of other sorts among children. In my view, the biblical, theological and developmental evidence suggests that these latter are more appropriate for adults. In saying this, I am aware that there will be those who have witnessed the exercise of a charismatic-style vocal phenomena by children and who will therefore reject my arguments. To them I can only say the following: (a) I do not rule out the exceptional or occasional use of such spiritual gifts by children but I do question whether they should ever be promoted as normative or that children should be pushed to expect them as part of what it means to follow Christ; (b) the balance of theological evidence suggests we should be wary about associating these gifts with children as a rule; (c) even if the theological questions could be adequately dealt with, the developmental questions still remain and cannot be wished away; and (d) current fears for the well-being of children are a new factor that must be taken seriously and not dismissed as somehow irrelevant or unspiritual.

Notes to *appendix 2*

1   Ishmael (Ian Smale) argues that children should be encouraged to receive and exercise spiritual gifts as a routine matter of discipleship. However, for the reasons cited throughout this chapter, I believe this to be mistaken. See Ian Smale (Ishmael), *Angels with Dirty Faces: Children in the Kingdom of God*, Eastbourne, Kingsway 1989, pp64-66. I am grateful to Emma Phillips for this reference.

2   C K Barrett, *The First Epistle to the Corinthians*, London, A & C Black, 1973, p279.

3   Barrett, as above, p281.

4   John Wimber, *Power Evangelism*, London, Hodder & Stoughton, 1985, p46.

# Afterword

We have reached the end of this book but not of our learning. As our ministry to children moves on, we shall, if we are attentive to the Spirit of God, be always ready to discern new insights and revise old ones. This is perhaps especially true as new generations come of age in the wake of the Millennium. But as we close this study, I should like to set out three convictions which have been central throughout and which have grown in strength as I have continued writing:

1. Children are infinitely precious to God

This is not just a piece of the sentimentality which characterises modern attitudes to children. It is a hard theological fact: the Son of God gave himself for the sons and daughters of men so that they might become children of God. The incarnation of Jesus as both child and adult underlines the commitment and identification of the eternal God with all the phases of our human growth and development. Jesus was child as well as man.

2. We have a tremendous responsibility to fulfil

If God has acted in love towards children, then so must we. We must never regard them merely as miniature adults or souls to win. They are persons, each in his or her own right, and each made in God's image. This does not mean we have to be indulgent or naive: children too share in human flawedness and sin. But our responsibility is to love, cherish and care. As a result we shall be careful never to manipulate young minds or hearts, even from the best of intentions. As adults we shall be conscious both of their vulnerability and of our power. Our evangelism will reflect our awareness that we are not more than stewards of the gospel and shepherds of God's flock. We are not sheepdogs whose purpose is to round children up into the pen of our own making. God will not thank us for that.

3. God has entrusted us with the task of understanding

This will involve a willingness to grapple with both theology and child development. The easiest thing in the world would now be to put this book down and go back to ministry as if nothing had changed. Only when we struggle with trying to match with our experience the difficult questions thrown up by the study of child development, and then try to think about both theologically, will we find that God opens our hearts and minds to something new. If we are determined that we have nothing new to learn then God will simply let us be confirmed in our refusal. If, however, we are ready humbly and honestly to bring ourselves and our questions to him, he will give us answers in due course. That is the conviction and message of this book.

Growing in Faith series

Three books for all those involved in children's evangelism. The books work together and complement each other, providing a 'head, heart and hands' approach to the subject of child faith development. Written by experts in their field, the series will equip churches with a comprehensive training resource for children's workers.

Children Finding Faith: *Exploring a child's response to God*
Rev Dr Francis Bridger

This revised, expanded version of a popular book examines accepted studies of child development alongside the theological issues relating to children. Children Finding Faith follows the development of two children from birth to adolescence, charting the characteristics of their emotional and spiritual growth. New chapters look at social context, the practical implications of children's work and worship.

£6.99, B format pb, 224 pp 1 85999 323 0 (SU) 1 902041 10 0 (CPAS)

Bringing Children to Faith: *Training adults in evangelism with children*
Penny Frank

This training manual will enable you to think through the principles of good practice for evangelism with children, and implement them in your children's work. In workbook format, Bringing Children to Faith contains photocopiable pages and suggestions for group discussion and activity. Use this resource to plan a series of workshops for your church children's team, a training day or to help you as you develop a whole church strategy for children's evangelism.

£7.50, A4, 48pp 1 85999 410 5 (SU) 1 8976 6093 6 (CPAS)

Mission Possible: *Ideas and resources for children's evangelism*
Various

Mission Possible is a ready-to-use resource book full of ideas and activities for use with children. Arranged in age-group sections, ranging from crèche through to early teens, activities are relevant to children's age and level of development. Drawn from the experience of Scripture Union and CPAS children's workers, these tried and tested activities will enable you to put into practice some of the ideas outlined in the other two books.

£7.50, A4, 64pp 1 85999 411 3 (SU) 1 902041 05 4(CPAS)

You can obtain any of the above books through your local Christian bookshop, via christianbookshop.com or (in the UK) direct from:

Scripture Union Mail Order PO Box 764 OXFORD OX4 5FJ Tel: **01865 716880** Fax: 01865 715152
CPAS Sales Athena Drive Tachbrook Park WARWICK CV34 6NG Tel/24 hour voicemail: **01926 458400**
For overseas sales, contact your national Scripture Union office.